It Takes a Worried Man

It
Takes a
Worried
Man

A MEMOIR

Brendan
Halpin

VILLARD
NEW YORK

Library of Congress Cataloging-in-
Publication Data
Halpin, Brendan.
It takes a worried man: a memoir/Brendan
Halpin.—1st ed.
p. cm.
ISBN 0-375-50716-7 (alk. paper)
1. Halpin, Brendan. 2. Shanks, Kirsten
Conant—Health. 3. Breast—Cancer—
Patients—United States—Biography. I. Title.

RC280.B8 H356 2001
362.1'9699449'0092—dc21
[B]   2001041907

Villard Books website address:
www.villard.com

Printed in the United States of America on
acid-free paper
24689753
First Edition
Book design by Jennifer Ann Daddio

It Takes a Worried Man

Kirsten told me I should write it all down. I think she thinks it will be good therapy for me. I have noticed that the stuff written about my situation is usually a line or two in the cancer books: "This is a tough time for him too." So maybe there is some room for my story. I begin this on October 7, 2000. Tomorrow is our sixth anniversary.

The Troll

Somehow, as much as I wish he weren't, the Troll feels like part of this story. We lived for four years in a condo over a childless couple: a Grizzly Adams–looking, dyspeptic folk singer and his wife. We'll leave the wife out of it, though she was a pain in the ass too. The husband, hereafter known as the Troll, is a loud-mouth bully—one of those guys who is angry all the time and never stops to consider the possibility that maybe it's not every-one else in the world who's an asshole.

After our daughter, Rowen, was born, he became convinced that we were torturing him by allowing our daughter to walk. Honestly. This despite the fact that *his* favorite hobby was rattling our floors with his own special brand of 1970s wuss-rock. His response to our completely unreasonable practice of allowing our offspring to move freely about our home got in-creasingly loony, culminating in him pounding on our door one Sunday morning and running away and then calling Kirsten a "stupid, ignorant, tight-lipped bitch" in front of our daughter the next day. He did his best to make selling our condo and moving out difficult, including squeezing 175 bucks in bogus "fines" from the condo association out of us. Our infractions included vacuuming at 9:00 A.M. and "heavy footfalls." Our lawyer told us the fines were bullshit and he'd be happy to fight them for us for two hundred dollars an hour. We paid the fines and sold the place for two and a half times what we'd paid for it. The Troll wrote "HA-HA-HA-HA-HA" on the back of the canceled check.

I never tried to take any revenge, figuring that getting into a lunacy contest with someone who has such a large head start is bad policy and that, you know, living well is the best revenge.

This has two implications for my story. One is that I took comfort in the knowledge that this hateful fuck would remain a hateful fuck and continue to find that the whole world was against him, while we would live happy lives in our new home.

The other implication is that we were busy moving all summer, and Kirsten decided to wait until her annual checkup in August to get those lumps in her right breast checked out.

Those Lumps

She had painful lumps in her right breast. A year earlier, she'd had an ultrasound for some other lumps and been told that they were nothing. So it was easy for her to blow these off and wait.

It wouldn't have been easy for me. I am a terrible hypochondriac. I worry constantly that every pain I have is a sign of a deadly disease, that my vision is blurring, that I have mad cow disease, that my pee is too bubbly, you name it. I also get chronic testicular inflammations. I had three ultrasounds on my nuts within six months because I was convinced I had testicular cancer. I mean, if your right nut feels like a bowling ball, that must mean something serious is wrong. Right?

Wrong, as it turns out. Sometimes my epididymis, which is a tube that carries sperm out of the testicle and sort of loops around it on the way out, gets inflamed. No big deal except, you know, my balls hurt a lot. C'est la vie.

Kirsten is always the steady one in these situations. She reassures me that I don't have testicular cancer, that I don't have mad cow disease, that my kidneys aren't failing. She is the voice of reason.

So when she said that those lumps were probably nothing, I didn't, you know, insist that she bust her ass into the doc's office because it could be serious. She wasn't concerned. I wasn't concerned.

My Crisis of Faith

My dad died when I was nine. He fell over dead for no apparent reason. Kind of like a grown-up version of a crib death. He was thirty-five. I'm now thirty-two. Now you know why I'm such a hypochondriac.

My parents had been raised Catholic, but had lapsed. I grew up with a terrible fear of dying and a kind of vague fear of hell informed mostly by my five visits to mass with relatives and some horror movies.

My mom returned to the Catholic Church when I was in college. I still remember getting this letter one day in which she said, "I have been going to mass every day." I was convinced she had lost her mind. Even Catholics think it's weird to go to mass every day. Nobody does that except for the priests, who have to, and old ladies.

Well, she hadn't lost her mind, and though now she only goes to mass weekly, the church has been a very positive force in her life. While she could return to the Catholic Church, I, who had never been in it, could not return. (I mean, yeah, they got me baptized just in case their parents had been right, but they stopped going to church about a week later. It doesn't seem like it counts, though if the Catholics are right, this ought to be enough to get me past limbo and into purgatory, assuming I don't do anything horrible between now and when I die.) I didn't know what to do. I had vague religious leanings and too much skepticism to profess belief in Christ's divinity or resurrection, both of which seem to me to be kind of beside the point of his message anyway, which I know is some kind of heresy. So, naturally, I became a Unitarian.

I have been going, more or less regularly, to the Wednesday night prayer group at my church. This is an unusually Christian kind of activity for Unitarians to engage in. We're much better at petition drives and protests. Not only do we say the "Our Father and Mother" (we are still Unitarians, after all), we also sort of chant the 23rd Psalm at the beginning, without even trying to correct for patriarchal language. The 23rd Psalm, by the way, is great. Thinking of yourself as a sheep being led around by a benevolent God is a pretty comforting thought when things are tough. I also like the end: "surely goodness and mercy shall follow me all the days of my life, and I will dwell in the house of the Lord forever." We'll see.

Though Emerson, the man who sort of runs the prayer group, is a spiritual superhero, and I do love everybody there, I found this summer that I was going less than I used to. While I like to pray, I need to go to group because I am too lazy to do it by myself. I started to have doubts, though. I know prayer makes me feel good, and I believe it's effective, but if God can intervene in the world, I guess I wonder why he doesn't do it more often. If God intervenes, where was he in Bosnia, Kosovo, Rwanda, etc. etc. etc.? Therefore God doesn't intervene. So why am I asking him to look out for people, or grant healing to people, or to bring somebody home safely? What am I doing? Does it matter? I think I have now officially become a Unitarian. I am too tied in knots intellectually to pray.

This crisis of faith comes before—*before,* mind you—the Diagnosis.

The Diagnosis

Kirsten went for her annual physical. When she came back, she said that her doctor had recommended that she go for another ultrasound. So she went. Rowen and I went too. We walked around the pond near the doctor's office looking at the geese and feeding them. Rowen picked up a stick and announced that it was a magic wand. There was goose shit everywhere, so we imagined that she could make it go away with her magic wand. "Zoop! No more poop!" she'd say. It was a beautiful summer day and I was happy.

Later I heard that they had found a dead bird carrying the West Nile virus very near to where Rowen and I had been walking. I worried about West Nile. Had I been bitten by a mosquito that day? Had Rowen?

The ultrasound came back inconclusive. The doc said something like, "It doesn't really look cancerous. It doesn't really look benign." Apparently it was round on one side, which is cystlike, and nubbly on the other side, which is cancerlike. So they set up an appointment with a surgeon who is some kind of breast specialist.

Weeks went by, as they always do when you are waiting to see a specialist. We unpacked, worked on the new house, stripped wallpaper, and made a million trips to the Home Depot.

The breast specialist looked at the ultrasound and decided to order a mammogram and a "needle biopsy." Here's where it started to get scary. But okay, you can still talk to ten women and probably five of them have had an ultimately benign lump in their breast biopsied.

I didn't go with her to the biopsy. It didn't seem important. It's just a formality. When they described the procedure to her, they said it was basically sticking a needle into the lump and sucking some cells out.

When she came home, her breast was bandaged, bruised, and bloody. She described how they had held this gunlike apparatus to her breast and fired it in nine times. They sent her home with this information sheet that said, "You may experience some oozing." All of a sudden, this felt real. I got incredibly sad when she undressed. It just looked like she'd been beaten up. I guess she had. I had to leave the room to cry, because I understood very clearly that my role was to be positive. This looked bad, though.

The biopsy was Friday morning before Labor Day weekend, so it was going to be Wednesday before we found anything out. We had dinner with some friends and had a very nice weekend.

School started that week. I am a teacher at a small charter high school in Boston. Tuesday was upper-class orientation. I met my advisees again—this is a group of kids that has the misfortune of having me as the person in charge of organizational stuff like filing their transcripts and presenting their grades to their parents, and the good fortune of having me as someone to listen to them and advocate for them. I suck at the organizational part of this job, and I have been very good at the advocate-counselor kind of parts. Anyway, it was nice to see my advisees again. I have a lot of affection for them even though many of them are chronic pains in the ass who are always in trouble because they can't stop themselves from saying something rude to a teacher or something.

Talking about this at the end of the day, Kirsten busts me. She says, "You love those kids more than the others." I protest that I really like and get along with all of my students, and she levels me with this: "There is a certain kind of kid that you like the best, and those are the smart troublemakers." She has me there.

Day two of school is the first day of classes. Things go well, except that I still don't have my office supplies. We are having some kind of dispute with Staples, so our supplies haven't arrived. I really need some pens and index cards, so I walk over to the college bookstore, which is about ten minutes away.

I carry a pager, but I have it in my pocket on this day. We don't let the kids carry them, and I sort of hate to have it on my belt proclaiming the hypocrisy of the adult world, so I keep it in my pocket. While I am walking to the bookstore, my pager vibrates, but because I am wearing these loose-fitting pants, I don't feel it.

I buy some pens and index cards. I head back to school in a leisurely way. I stop and talk to somebody in the faculty room. I eventually check my e-mail. I read and respond to about three messages. Then I open the one from the office manager, which says, "Your lovely wife has been trying to reach you. She is at the hospital. Please call her."

Well, that's it, isn't it? They only make you come to the hospital if they have bad news for you. They call you up and say, "Come in to discuss your results," because they don't want to tell you bad news on the phone, but of course they already have, because if they had good news, they would just say, "Your biopsy came back totally normal."

I duck into a room and call the number she's given me. It

rings and rings and rings and rings. I call home—no answer. I call the hospital again. It rings and rings and rings. What the hell kind of hospital is this? Are there no receptionists? Is there no voice mail? This endlessly ringing phone just seems ominous. I am on the verge of tears.

And then I see her through the door. Kirsten has come to school to find me. I see her smile at one of my co-workers— maybe it's not terrible news after all. She comes in the room and begins to sob. "I have cancer," she says. I hold her while she cries. "I'm so scared. I don't want to die."

"You won't," I tell her. "You won't."

Well, at Least It Can't Get Much Worse

We talk for a few more minutes, then she goes out to the car, while I head back into the room I share with five other teachers to grab my backpack and jacket. Practically everyone in this room is new to the school. Luckily Lisa, whom I have known for a year, is there. She looks at me, and I am about to cry. "Is everything okay?" she asks, and I sort of pull her back to the corner of the room.

"Kirsten has cancer," I sob, and she hugs me. "I don't know what I'm going to do. I'm not strong enough to do this. I can't lose her. I can't lose her." Lisa says reassuring things about how I am not going to lose her and I have lots of help, so I don't need to be strong all by myself. It's true. She will see me cry many more times before the treatment even starts.

I gather my stuff and leave, and the other people I share the room with politely pretend that they haven't heard and they aren't curious. This is a great kindness.

The plan, Kirsten explains, is for her to have a semiradical or total or, anyway, some kind of mastectomy that involves hacking her entire breast, and then some, off. Then a little radiation, a little chemo, and boom, she's better.

Of course, I am already worried about her dying. As much as I reassure her, it is just in my hypochondriac nature to imagine the worst. All I can think is, "How will I get Rowen to school?" and, "Oh my God, does this mean my mom will have to move in?"

She now needs to go for several tests to make sure the cancer hasn't spread. First they tell her she needs a bone scan. Then they say she needs a bone scan and a CAT scan. But they hadn't said that two days ago. Are they acting on some new information?

Why yes, as a matter of fact, they are. When Kirsten is reeling from the radioactive shake they made her drink, she runs into her breast specialist surgeon outside the hospital. The surgeon tells her that her bloodwork came back a little abnormal. Two of the tumor markers are elevated. I don't know what this means. I later find out that tumors not in the breast cause some kind of elevated hormone levels in your blood, so this is bad news. And they told her on the fucking street.

Kirsten's Parents

Kirsten's parents are dropping by the night we find out. They are on their way back from cleaning out some elderly relative's house in New Hampshire. They call from the road. Kirsten tells them.

They come over and we get hugs and stuff, but no tears are shed. This is okay. Kirsten's parents are lovely people, but they just don't really operate on the level of deep emotions. That is to say, I have seen them annoyed and happy, but after ten years I don't really know what makes them sad or what they are afraid of. That stuff is just not on public display. This makes them fairly easy to hang out with. You can pretty much be guaranteed that any long-simmering resentments are not ever going to boil over. They will just stay simmering close to forever.

This is a marked contrast to my mom, who never lets anything simmer for very long. Any kind of resentment needs to bubble up almost immediately. This also makes her kind of easy to hang out with, because she never hides anything. Aside from the fact that real or imagined conflicts often lead to painful, meaningful talks about the state of our relationship, we get along fine.

Anyway, Kirsten's folks take the news pretty hard, I think. You can't really tell by how they conduct themselves, but they start remodeling our house with a vengeance. Her dad had been helping us redo the staircase up to the attic, which was ugly and poorly constructed. When he took it apart we found that the whole thing had been balanced on basically three nails. I thought about the surly Israeli guys who moved us in and how many times they stomped up those steps and it seemed like a miracle nobody fell to their death.

Moldings are finished. A power miter saw is purchased. Missing balusters are tracked down and replaced. Much drywalling, plastering, and painting goes on around the area of the new staircase. The new staircase is so solidly built that five Israeli movers with crowbars probably couldn't get it down.

I appreciate the impulse. They want to do something to help, and this feels good and tangible. And it does help.

You Should Already Be Dead

It has been, to put it mildly, a real bitch of a week. On top of everything else, Kirsten had to take an indefinite leave from her job teaching refugees how to get and keep jobs in hotels. The money, luckily, is not an issue because our Troll-free home is a multifamily and the rents cover our mortgage, but it is a real psychological blow to both of us for her to have to stop working. Welcome to the Land of the Critically Ill.

Doctor Sensitive, Ms. "Your Tumor Markers Are Elevated, Oh, There's My Bus," calls on Friday night. She says to Kirsten, "I think there was some mistake in your bloodwork. If your potassium level is this high, you should already be dead. I'm sure it's a mistake, but you need to go to the emergency room right away and have it retested."

I had really been looking forward to kicking back with a beer and a sporting event, but it was not to be. I had also been looking forward to a calm, uneventful year of working on the house and the yard. But what the hell are you going to do.

So off we go to the emergency room. I drop Kirsten off and Rowen and I head off to this amazing and really cheap Mexican place about ten minutes' walk from the hospital. On the way over to dinner, I end up talking to Rowen about what's happening, about how mom is going to have surgery (I show her my appendectomy scar to sort of illustrate the concept of surgery) and then she'll need to come back to the hospital for treatment, and how that will involve her getting some really strong medicine that is going to make her feel crappy for a while but will eventually make her better.

I get through this okay, though I almost start to cry when I realize that some passer-by is listening to us. We get to the restaurant and eat outside and watch people heading over to the Red Sox game. It's a practically perfect night. We go to the playground across the street after dinner. As strange as it sounds, it is a wonderful, wonderful night.

We walk back to the hospital and find Kirsten in an examining room behind the emergency room. She seems to be in pretty good spirits. "The doctor's name is Nancy Drew," she whispers to me after the emergency room doctor walks out. "I haven't made any girl-detective jokes. I was very tempted to ask her about Ned, but I decided I didn't want to annoy her." I would never be able to be so strong. But keeping quiet is the best course of action. What kind of Nancy Drew joke do you think you could come up with that she hasn't already heard?

So Nancy Drew comes in and says the lab boys have their shorts all bunched up and don't understand how this happened and want to study Kirsten's blood as some kind of freak of science, but basically her potassium level is fine, her heart hasn't stopped, she's not dead.

Then she says, "Do you have any other health problems?"

We both laugh. Nancy Drew looks hurt, but I keep laughing. It is the funniest thing I have heard all week.

The Multi Disappointment

Somebody calls Kirsten and says, "You have a multi disappointment on Thursday." She eventually figures out that this is oncology lingo for "multidisciplinary appointment." The first reading seems a lot more in line with everything we've experienced so far. It is to be a two-hour appointment, and I get out of work right at the end of school so as to make the second hour.

I could have probably left earlier and made the first hour too, but that would have involved getting a sub for my afternoon class. Leaving work in any way cuts into my little wall of denial, and I hate that. I like going to work and just forgetting that anything is happening.

The multi disappointment really really blows. We sit in the fucking room for really long periods of time waiting for people to show up. The radiation guy is incredibly lugubrious. He makes all these vague statements, like, "Well, of course, if the cancer has spread, as we think it may have because of these test results, then the objective of the treatment changes." Well what exactly the fuck does that mean? If the objective of the treatment is currently to save her life, then what's the new objective?

The nurse, on the other hand, is extremely chipper. I want to smack her. We spend forty-five minutes waiting for Maryann, the oncologist, who is very nice and extremely attractive, and she tells us nothing new at all.

The thing that really pisses me off, that makes me want to slap the whole bunch of them, is the fact that they just can't hide it: fundamentally, they are scientists, and they want all their data to make sense. Right now they have one piece of data that doesn't make sense, and it's driving them nuts. They *want* it to have spread. That way their test makes sense. Bastards.

What the CAT Scan Said

The day after the multi disappointment, Kirsten is told that they found something on her CAT scan. It is a spot on her spine. They don't know exactly what it is.

This is not good news.

Kirsten is pretty much beside herself. She pages me, but I am already in the subway station. I am now wearing my pager on my belt and enduring the kids' taunts about my hypocrisy with stoicism and the occasional, "Lay off, because if I tell you why I have this, you're going to feel bad."

I call her up.

"Where are you?" she asks. I can tell by her tone of voice that something is wrong.

"I'm in the subway station."

"Okay, then just come home and I'll tell you when you get here."

"Is everything okay?"

"Just . . . just come home. I just had a bad conversation with Maryann."

It takes a very long twenty minutes to get home.

When I walk inside she starts to cry. I hold her, and she tells me that she is tired, just so tired of getting bad news. I am too. She is a little confused about the news—she sort of stopped processing after the initial information—so I call Maryann, the oncologist.

Here are some highlights of our conversation:

"Well, we see this spot on one of her vertebrae. It could be something we call a bone island, which is something we see on CAT scans from time to time and we don't know exactly what they are and we only gave them a name because we kept seeing them on CAT scans."

This sounds like good news to me. I am getting hopeful.

"But," she continues, "this doesn't really look characteristic of one of those."

Shit. "Does it," I say, "look characteristic of cancer?"

"Well, no. We don't really know what it is. The MRI and the PET scan should tell us for sure."

The PET scan does not find out if you should have a dog, by the way. It involves being shot up with radioactive glucose, which tumor cells for some reason like a lot more than regular cells, so when the technicians take some kind of picture of you, the tumor cells glow brighter. Or something.

She goes on to say that we are still assuming that she will have a mastectomy in a week and a half, but we will need to see from the results of the tests next week. If the tests show that the spot is cancerous, then the surgery is off, because, basically, what's the point. See, it turns out that breast cancer in the actual breast never kills anybody. Makes sense, because if you needed breasts to live, they couldn't very well cut them off. It's only when it gets out that it kills you, usually by going after your liver. So if Kirsten's is out of the barn, so to speak, there is no sense in trying to shut the gate and "the objective of the treatment changes."

I decide to go for the big question. "So if this is metastatic," I say, "is that a death sentence? Because that's what we're hearing."

Beat.

Beat.

Beat.

I have prepared meals in less time than it takes for her to answer this. "Well," she starts out, "there are some very special patients—I mean, we are talking about the Louis Armstrong of cancer patients—" This analogy annoys me somehow. I don't know why. Couldn't she say the Michael Jordan of cancer patients? Maybe the Eddie Van Halen of cancer patients? The, um, Pedro Martinez? I don't know. I am not very familiar with Satchmo's oeuvre, so I find this annoying. "—who respond very well to treatment and can live relatively normal lives for years."

"When you say that the objective of the treatment is different, what exactly do you mean? Are we talking about pain abatement, or are we talking about fighting the disease?"

"Oh, we are absolutely fighting this disease," she says emphatically. I think she is horrified that I suggested that they sounded like they were giving up after they basically said they were giving up for two days. She goes on to say that while this would be bad news, it would be the best bad news possible, since these spots are tiny, and she has nothing wrong with her liver. Somehow I manage to come away from the conversation with the idea that she could live ten years with this treatment. I figure if ten, why not twenty or thirty? You are always hearing about these people: "The doctors told her she had a year to live, and twenty-five years later, she is fine . . ." I write a quote from Maryann in big letters in the cancer notebook: BAD BUT FIGHTABLE. I feel optimistic. Sort of.

Our Romantic Weekend

That conversation takes place late Friday afternoon, and Kirsten's mom has taken Rowen away for the weekend so that we can have some time to just be together. It is a nice gesture.

With Rowen out of the house, I was hoping for some hot sex this weekend, but this news makes it appear unlikely. Kirsten is really depressed, and I go into full cheerleader mode. We go out for dinner and to a movie. It is a nice night, but it is totally tainted by this new news. It is fun, but not carefree.

After the movie, we walk back to the subway, and after a pause in our conversation, she says, "If I die, you can't remarry."

"Ever?"

"Ever. I'll haunt you."

I pause to digest this. "Can I have a string of meaningless affairs with twenty-four-year-olds?"

She pauses to digest that. "Okay. But Rowen can never find out."

I think I can live within these parameters.

I have to confess I have already been thinking about this stuff. I know I would be a wreck. I am already kind of a wreck. I have left out a lot of my conversations with my friends at work and on the phone after Kirsten goes to bed. Well, calling them conversations is really a whitewash. They involve me sobbing, "I can't lose her, I can't lose her," while they pat my shoulder and tell me it's going to be okay. Or say on the phone that they wish they could give me a hug and that it's going to be okay.

But I would be tragic, and therefore probably a babe magnet. I can brood with the best of them. Also, I'm good with kids. I figure if you just take those points, I could probably get laid.

But I also know that I wouldn't want to. All I would want to do is cry and listen to country music. In fact, that's much of what I want to do now.

Anyway, we go out to breakfast the next day. We rent some movies. We go out to lunch. We watch whatever Kirsten wants on TV. She commandeers the remote, saying, "I have cancer! I get to watch what I want!" And we do end up having sex, and it is some of the hottest sex we have had in a long time.

Those of you who are married may know what I mean. There is, you know, standard sex, which is wonderful and nothing to sneeze at and which I am not in any way putting down. But then, sometimes, at unpredictable times, you recover that passion from when you were dating, and then instead of, "I love you, sweetie," you have, "Oh my God I must have you now! And then, possibly, again!"

Anyway, there is nothing like staring into the void to spice up the old sex life, and we go after each other hungrily. It feels like a way of denying this whole horrible nightmare, and I guess maybe it sort of is. To engage in the procreative act is about the only way we have of defying death. You might get me, but by God I'm going to leave some DNA behind, you fucker.

Mind you, we are very careful that this act does not have the potential to result in actual procreation.

In any case, by the end of the weekend, we are in a pretty okay mental state and not just because of the sex, although it certainly didn't hurt.

I'm a Jackass Too

At some point during the initial weeks, Kirsten turns to me and says, "So are you going to have an affair?" I just have nothing to say except, "No. Why on earth would you say that?"

I am flabbergasted not because she's read my mind but because having an affair is probably the furthest thing from my mind. I work next to a large university, and I walk through campus before and after work on the way to the subway. I always enjoy ogling the undergraduate cuties, but after Kirsten's diagnosis I am sort of repulsed by the twenty-year-olds in their skintight tank tops. All I can think is, "Jesus, look at them lugging those cancer bags around."

So Kirsten's inquiry strikes me as really odd. She follows up with, "They say a lot of men do." And I am once more embarrassed to be a man. What kind of jackass runs around on his wife at a time like this? This comes after the initial diagnosis period when every medical professional she came in contact with seemed mildly surprised to find that she had a "supportive husband." She said they told her, "a lot of men aren't."

I can't help but feel contempt for these guys. What the hell do you think your marriage is if you can't support your wife when she's fighting for her life? I just sort of imagine these guys being like, "Okay, good luck with the mastectomy, hon, I'll be playing golf."

Well, it only takes a few days before I understand the jackasses a little better. I am back to ogling the undergraduate cuties, and while I am not about to have an affair, I sort of understand why men do it. Wouldn't it be nice to have something in my life that was just easy and fun? Right now everything is really really hard, and even the fun stuff seems to have a cloud over it. (Yes, I imagine knowing that you were cheating on your critically ill spouse might cast a pall over the adulterous proceedings, but I guess you never know.)

I also understand how people do it. I have always thought that I would be a horrible adulterer—basically she would know the second I got home because I am a terrible liar. But I am getting better. In fact, for the first time in my life, I am engaged in a large-scale pattern of deception, hiding huge chunks of my emotional life from Kirsten. I am usually unable to hide anything, to a degree that gets annoying, but now I am worried all the time, I am incredibly sad, I am terrified of losing her, but I can't let any of this stuff show at home. I have to be positive, because *she* has to believe that she can beat this disease, and in order for her to believe this, I have to believe it. And I do. But there is a whole other side of my life that I now must conceal.

So should I ever decide to have an affair, I now possess one of the essential skills. I have learned how to lie to my wife.

I sort of hate to go home at the end of the day now. At work, I can just worry about work, and I am trying to mediate these ridiculous conflicts about who said what about whose boyfriend, and then I have to go home and face the reality of what's happening. And the reality really really sucks. I don't play golf, but if I did, I might go for a few rounds right about now.

And Speaking of a Few Rounds

When we first get the news, I joke that I can't decide between alcoholism and overeating as a coping strategy. I get a lot of mileage out of the joke, though most people don't respond with the gales of laughter I would like. I guess they're not sure if I'm joking. Neither am I.

I do ramp up my alcohol consumption, but just to basically one drink a night. Except on those nights when I buy a bottle of wine, which is about once a week, and I can never seem to have less than two glasses. This is moderate drinking by almost anyone's standards, and really not so different from my pre-diagnosis intake. Except now I need it more. On days when we are out of beer I will make sure that I have a beer in the house, even paying the exorbitant prices of the pizza shop/liquor store down the street if I have to. I am a little nervous about this, but it seems to be under control.

I am very wary of my alcohol intake. My maternal grandfather is an alcoholic, not to mention a mean, sociopathic sonofabitch. And, you know, my ethnic background is Irish. I know how much an alcoholic can screw up a family because most of my extended family is kind of screwed up in one way or another. This is not something I want to do to Kirsten and Rowen.

So if my drinking is under control, my eating is not. I have even more diabetes than alcoholism in my family, so I have been making an effort to lay off the sweets for quite some time. That all goes out the window. So does moderating my portion size and basically anything else involving not abusing food.

I am straining at the 34-inch waist of the pants I just bought a month ago. I have never worn more than a 33 before. I hope I don't end up a whale, but it is hard to beat food as a source of comfort. I have been walking forty-five minutes to work every day, and that is helping, but I feel myself getting sluggish and tubby. And I am not sure how to stop.

Salvation Through Electronics

As soon as this all begins, I start thinking about all of the things I can buy to make it better. "I'll get a CD burner," I say, "and then I can make you CDs to listen to while you're recovering from surgery and getting your chemo."

"Do you think you might like a Game Boy? Then you can play Tetris while you get your chemo . . ."

"Maybe we should get a new computer so you can e-mail everybody while you're laid up at home."

"I'm thinking I should get a cell phone, so you can reach me any time." I am still smarting from the pager debacle on the day of the diagnosis.

Kirsten nixes most of this stuff, and I know deep down—no actually, I know just below the surface—that it's pretty stupid. I just feel like if I could buy something, I could have some kind of control. You know, you give them the money and they give you the stuff. On a fundamental level, it makes sense in a way that getting cancer when you are thirty-two does not. It just makes the universe seem a little less random.

Kirsten is wiser than me and doesn't really want stuff. I keep trying, though. I scan the circulars in the Sunday paper, watching for the prices of the CD burners to go down, I scan the cell phone ads looking for a good deal, and I pretty much give up on the whole Game Boy idea. I just want to do something to make it better.

I decide that I will shave my head when she loses her hair. This feels like a tangible thing I can do. I am attracted by a three-day, sixty-mile walk for breast cancer that will be taking place nearby. I look at the Web site obsessively at work for about two days. I am put off by an article in one of my lefty magazines about how so much of the money goes to promotion, and by the fact that all the pictures on the Web site are of women. This would be okay—I seem to get along with women easier than men, and walking in this thing seems like the kind of sensitive-guy thing that women love, so I could probably have some nice flirtatious conversations, but all the women are in their fifties and sixties, and it just seems like spending three days with everybody's mom might not be the most fun I could have. Also it costs fifty-five bucks to register.

Of course, I am already helping Kirsten, just by being there, listening to her, being positive, and getting up with Rowen when she has to pee in the middle of the night. But buying stuff is easy, and this business of being a positive support is very hard.

It Takes a Worried Man

Early into this ordeal, I buy two CDs that prove incredibly helpful. One is *The Essential Johnny Cash,* three CDs worth, and the other is some British import of twenty-five essential Carter Family songs. The Carter Family are not Jimmy, Rosalynn, Chip, and Amy, but rather Sara, A.P., and Maybelle, and these recordings from the 1920s, 1930s, and 1940s are, in most people's opinion, pretty much the bedrock on which country music is built.

I know what you're thinking—corny-ass fat guys in stupid hats. But the thing is that this is not like that at all. It is simple, moving, and demented. The songs are about death, jilted lovers and death, and Jesus and death. It's very close-to-the-bone kind of stuff, and it really speaks to me during this time. You would think that I would want to listen to something a little more cheery, but Johnny Cash really ripping through the live version of "Folsom Prison Blues" is about as cheery as I can stand right now. Mostly I rely on the Carter Family singing about love, death, and Jesus. I guess this stuff just feels closer to where I am right now than anything else. I try with some of my old favorites, but the punk rock I loved as a teen doesn't really help with this angst the way it helped me deal with my angst over why a chubby sarcastic kid with braces couldn't get a date. (Funny, but it really was a mystery to me at the time.)

So it's the Carter Family, asking to be buried beneath the weeping willow, or saying that it takes a worried man to sing a worried song. Nobody sings "I will survive" at the end of a love affair in this world. They kill themselves, mostly, though sometimes they kill the other person too. The whole thing is just sort of suffused with death. I guess this comes from living close to the edge. I get a book out of the library and find that A.P. and Sara literally lived in a place called Poor Valley. I guess when you are shit poor and Appalachian, you make music that doesn't mess around with niceties. Right now I like that.

What I also like is that there is a rock-solid certainty about God's goodness and ultimate power to make everything okay that is in marked contrast to the murderous and suicidal proceedings of the other songs and that I wish I shared. If I can't quite bring myself to believe that everything is going to be okay, I can at least have Maybelle Carter saying, "Let us trust in our savior always/who keepeth everyone in his care."

This music is so wonderful that I wonder how its descendants, country music and folk music, came to suck so bad. How did we get from the power and weirdness of the Carter Family to Faith Hill's lite-rock ballads and the Indigo Girls complaining about how difficult it is to be a college student?

Maybe you have to be shit poor and Appalachian to make

this kind of music. And maybe you have to be walking through the valley of the shadow of death to really like it.

The MRI

The Tuesday after our romantic weekend, Kirsten is scheduled for an MRI to determine what the spot on her spine is. It is at six o'clock at night, which seems kind of strange to me, but it's also nice because the whole family gets to go. The hospital is not far from where I work. In fact, I will come to know this route really well. Three trolley stops and a five-minute walk, and I am there.

We are meeting at the hospital at 5:30, so I go to the over-priced natural foods supermarket near where I work beforehand to get an array of prepared foods. There are potato pancakes involved. Maybe it's my ethnic heritage, but pretty much nothing says comfort to me like potatoes and oil.

Anyway, I put all of this food into my backpack and head over to the hospital. It's cold and rainy. When I get there, I see Kirsten and Rowen in the waiting room, smiling and talking. We eat our food quickly. I eat too much. Still, it is kind of fun— it's like a little adventure, eating dinner in this basically empty hospital foyer. We are in good spirits. I, for one, am convinced that the MRI will give us good news about the spot on her spine.

As it gets close to six, we go down to the basement, which is where the "MRI suite" is. It is a dingy little room at the end of a dingy little hallway. There are a bunch of lockers there, and there are also some toys. The only magazine they have is *Modern Ra-*

diologist or some other crappy trade journal. I have no idea if this is part of a pattern of cost-cutting, or what, but there is just such a shitty magazine selection in all of these places. And it seems like the deeper you get into this process, the shittier the magazine selection gets. Kirsten's primary care doctor's waiting room is lavishly appointed with recent magazines. The oncology suite has like three two-year-old copies of *Sports Illustrated.* The MRI suite has one copy of a magazine nobody wants to read. I pick it up anyway—it is a year old.

But there are the toys, and there is also a TV, so maybe I shouldn't complain about the magazine selection. I turn on *Arthur,* and Rowen and I start playing some game that involves her hiding toys in lockers and me pretending to be mystified about their whereabouts. It is kind of fun.

Some lady in hospital employee clothes comes and plops down there in the waiting room. Without so much as asking, she flips the TV over to *World News Tonight.* I don't really mind, because Rowen and I were not really watching the TV, but still, it seems kind of crappy that she didn't even ask.

It soon becomes clear that this is an employee lounge, not a patient waiting room. The first woman stays for about fifteen minutes, then leaves. She never so much as looks at us or acknowledges our presence. Right after she leaves, I turn the TV back to *Arthur,* and then another employee comes in. He sits down, takes out the paper, and starts to read. Once *Arthur* ends, I ask Rowen if she wants to check out the newborn channel, but for some reason the TV keeps turning off before I get to the hospital nursery-cam channel. Finally the guy says, "Oh, what are you trying to watch?" I tell him I was trying to have a look at the babies so my daughter could see, but I'm not having any luck. "Oh," he says, "do you mind if I turn on the news?"

Well, it clearly is the employee break room. After all, he's probably here every night, and with luck, we'll never be here again. I tell him it's okay, and it is. As I said, we weren't watching it, and I did very much appreciate the fact that he asked.

I feel like a cup of coffee, so I convince Rowen that we should go to the cafeteria. We wind our way through several basement corridors. Hospital basements are creepy under the best of circumstances, but deserted at night—even at 7:00 P.M.— they give me a serious case of the willies. Luckily Rowen is not fazed at all, and she notices a lot more than I do. "Look at the guy on the door! He has a smiley face!" Someone has graffitied a smiley face on the male icon on the men's room door. "Look at the pretty pipes! They're so colorful!" Some exposed pipes above our head have been painted a rainbow of bright colors.

We get to the cafeteria, which at least has windows, and it is deserted. This makes no sense to me at all. It's only seven o'clock, and the hospital is always open. Where is everybody? I don't know, but I get my coffee and Rowen gets some cheesy popcorn, and we sit next to the window having our snacks and watching the cars go by in the rain outside. It is always nice to be inside drinking a hot beverage on a cold rainy night, but more than that, at the risk of getting pukey, even in a dismal hospital basement, even with the most important woman in both our lives down some hallway lying in a cold machine, it is calming, comforting, and wonderful for me to just sit here in Rowen's company.

Maryann

Two days after the MRI, we have our big meeting with Maryann, Kirsten's oncologist. Somewhere in there she has the PET scan— I guess that happens the day after the MRI. I didn't go, so I don't really remember. Anyway, I leave school early and hit the trolley, three stops, then walk five minutes to the hospital. I stop at the Starbucks in the lobby and get a small something. The counter person looks at me funny when I ask for a small coffee, but I just can't bring myself to call it tall or grande or double petite or whatever the hell they want me to call a small coffee.

I take my coffee upstairs to the cancer floor. We sit in the waiting room. We make some jokes, because that's what we do, but we are both nervous. I look down at the field hockey players across the street. There is a small women's college down there, and they have their soccer and field hockey teams out. It looks like it's just practice. In fact, the field hockey players are looking really pathetic—bad passing, bad shooting—we figure they must be JV.

Maryann eventually comes out. You can tell this is a serious appointment because she is only fifteen minutes late. She takes us back to an examining room and tells us that Kirsten has stage four cancer. She says she is saddened but not surprised by the PET scan and MRI that show the spots (first they told us there was one—now it turns out there are seven) on her spine to be cancerous.

Now, I haven't been doing any research on cancer or anything, but even I know that stage four is fucking terrible news. I was somehow feeling optimistic after my long conversation with Maryann on the phone when she told me if this news came that it was bad but fightable.

Well, apparently Maryann has a pretty strange definition of fightable. She talks in averages, which don't really mean anything, but I hear things like "eighteen months" and "three years." I am pretty sure that three years is how long Kirsten might expect to live with treatment. Maryann says things about HER-2/neu receptors, Herceptin, and the fact that promising treatments are in the pipeline. Fuck the pipeline. What the hell do you mean, three years? She's not even sick.

She also tells us about the "aggressive" treatment. This involves high doses, like ten times the standard doses, of chemotherapy, which completely destroy your immune system, so they have to suck out your immune-making cells beforehand, and they freeze them and reinject them after. There are all kinds of heinous side effects in addition to the immune system destruction. Maryann says that once you've had your immune system destroyed, you have to spend a month in the hospital, and no children under six are allowed to visit, because, you know, they are little germ factories.

This is hard to take. Rowen is very attached to Kirsten. I mean, well, duh, but Kirsten is definitely still the number one parent. Rowen and I have nice times together, but she prefers Kirsten. I can't imagine what she's going to be like if she can't see her mom for a month. Not to mention how is Kirsten going to fight for her life and try to keep her will to live through horrible nausea without Rowen there to encourage her with hugs and drawings and stuff? This really sucks.

I say something like, "Well, I suppose it would be worth it to have her in the hospital for a month and to have worse side effects if we could have her for another ten years." I am quoting, remember, a number of years that I swear Maryann told me Kirsten could have if she was Louis Armstrong or Tiger Woods or Yo-Yo Ma.

And Maryann looks at me and says, "I can't talk about ten years." What do you mean, you can't talk about ten years? You mean it's hopeless? You mean I'm going to be widowed by the time I'm forty-two? How can you possibly be telling me this? How can this be true? It's barely even out of her breast, some tiny spots on her spine and you're telling me some bullshit about three years? You can't talk about ten years? Well I can talk about ten years, goddammit. I can talk about fifteen or twenty. Where the fuck does she get off telling me I can't have Kirsten forever?

Maryann talks and talks and talks but I pretty much stop hearing her. She talks in circles: she will talk about treatment option A, then option B, then B some more with an aside about A, then back to A with an aside about B, and after an hour it becomes impossible to follow her. I do remember her saying, though, that this aggressive treatment is very controversial in the breast cancer world, and lots of people, including every other hospital in town, think it is basically quackery and akin to throwing a pig off the roof to teach it to fly—doesn't work and it's cruel to the pig. I swear she says this. And Kirsten is the pig.

Well, I can no longer absorb what Maryann is talking about,

so I just kind of look at her and think about how she's a very attractive woman. Yes, if you needed further confirmation that men are assholes and that I am one of them, I swear I sat there thinking about how foxy my wife's oncologist was.

Pretty damn foxy, in case you were wondering.

Dr. J

The day after our meeting with Maryann, we go back for a meeting with Dr. J, who runs the "aggressive" treatment program. Her name is Joan, but we call her Dr. J because, you know, she is this heavyset white lady and looks nothing like Julius Erving. What can I say, it's funny to us.

Dr. J is scheduled to leave the country tomorrow, but she kind of sneaks onto the cancer floor just to see us. I once again have to leave work early. I have spent much of the time I should have spent correcting papers and preparing for my classes looking at stuff on the Internet about bone marrow transplants for breast cancer, and the stuff I have found is sort of semi-reassuring. I read some article from like 1987 by Stephen Jay Gould about how he got diagnosed with some wacky cancer that they told him the average patient lived with for eight months from diagnosis, but he did all this research and, being a scientist, understood something about statistics, which is more than most of the people I know who ever took a statistics class, and he figured the average didn't mean squat when it came to him, and he is still alive, so I guess he was right. I found an infamous study about bone marrow transplants that showed that there is no benefit at all in the survival time from this treatment. Then there was some other thing I no longer remember that they did with five people in France, and the results were preliminary but encouraging. Or something.

At any rate, they are still acting like we have a choice here between the standard and the aggressive treatment, but the nomenclature alone gives it away. Faced with something that could kill you, do you want to take it in a standard way, or do you want to go after it aggressively? Well, who's going to reject aggressive? It seems like the path of hope.

While I was incredibly depressed after our meeting with Maryann, Dr. J is much more positive and upbeat. She also speaks much more clearly: while Maryann spoke in these crazy circles, listening to Dr. J is like reading an outline. We proceed from one treatment to another, and every side effect is explained in detail, times are outlined, and I follow the whole thing from start to finish, which is three hours in one of these windowless exam rooms. It probably doesn't hurt that I don't find Dr. J attractive at all, so I am not distracted by that as I was when we talked to Maryann.

Anyway, by the end of this, we have all but made up our minds to go with Dr. J's patented restorative tonic, which is another joke we have about this being some kind of experimental snake oil treatment. Apparently fifteen percent of patients get a complete remission (which is not, they are quick to tell us, a cure) from the standard treatment. Dr. J says that they have been getting sixty percent of patients with a complete remission in this aggressive treatment program. Basically the side effects are going to be horrific, but for an overall shorter period of time.

The idea with this treatment is that you undergo this nightmarish ordeal for a few months and are then done. With the standard treatment, the ordeal is less nightmarish, but it's never really over—you just basically bounce from one treatment to the next. Dr. J tells us that some small percentage of patients are symptomatic when they do their first round of chemo, meaning that their cancer is in some way impacting their ability to live a normal life in some way other than the psychological sword of Damocles kind of way. The majority of people are symptomatic by their second round, everybody is symptomatic by their third round, and nobody gets a fourth round.

Dr. J says that she has various appointments lined up for Kirsten, but she is free to cancel them, and that she supports whatever decision we make. She also says to me that she could not do her job without thinking about being in the other chair, and she knows what she would do if she were in Kirsten's place, and she knows exactly what the side effects look like because she treats people all the time who are going through them. That is a powerful statement, but really our minds were made up before. Who wouldn't want to fight?

We have known Dr. J for several years because she goes to our church, and I know her to be a very good and deeply spiritual person. She once thought she wanted to be a minister, and she is certainly ministering to us right now. I feel good about having her in charge.

I Love the Dead

Soon after our epic meetings with Maryann and Dr. J, I feel this powerful need to rent living dead movies. Actually, I get this urge periodically, but every time I wave one of the movie boxes at Kirsten in the video store, she says, "No *way* are we renting that," then proceeds to show me the box of some three-hour heartwarming tale of a Chinese peasant woman's tenacious struggle to bring in the wheat harvest or something, which I similarly nix.

This week, though, I will not be denied. I go to the video store and have to root around, but I eventually find what I am looking for. *Dead Alive,* which is a demented tale from New Zealand about a meek mama's boy whose life is changed forever when his domineering mother is bitten by a Sumatran rat monkey and transformed into a zombie. This film features pus squirting into custard which is then consumed, a priest who says, "I kick ass for the Lord," and an incredible climax where the aforementioned mama's boy hacks through dozens of zombies with a lawn mower. Did I mention the evil zombie baby and the blender?

I also rent *Evil Dead 2,* which is a better-known classic involving a creepy cabin filled with flesh-eating spirits who squeal, "I'll swallow your soul!," an eyeball which pops out of somebody's head and into somebody else's mouth, and a hand that turns evil and attacks its owner while it is still attached.

Kirsten has never seen either movie, and I insist that she do so. So we watch both movies, and they are just as wonderful as I remember. We laugh our asses off as body parts are hacked off left and right, blood spurts, and bad acting rules.

I suppose it doesn't take Sigmund Freud to figure out that there is something going on here about mocking death, that having a laugh as a disembodied head bites somebody in the crotch is really about trying to defy the death that waits for us all and that is currently menacing Kirsten in a way that makes me want to wallop it. Whatever the case, I find these movies immensely more comforting than anything that has those quotes on the box that say, "wise, witty, and wonderful," or "inspiring and uplifting."

Cold Kirkin'

There is some episode of the old *Star Trek* where Captain Kirk, for reasons I don't remember, but that probably involved him getting freaky with some alien babe, starts moving through time at a different rate than the rest of his crew. So he is there on the Starship *Enterprise,* and he can see everybody, but they can't see him because he's moving too fast, and they appear like frozen statues to him.

I think about this episode a lot these days. I frequently feel like Captain Kirk—I can see everybody, but they can't see me. I occupy the same space as everybody else, but we are having completely different experiences. I ride the subway with them, I see them at work, and they are worried about the paper they have due, or they are excited about a movie, or whatever—they are just concerned with the wonderful mundane shit that is everyday life. And I am sitting right next to them watching them from another reality. They may as well be frozen for all that I can relate to them. Kirk, as I remember, was kind of tortured by his experience and wanted nothing more than to be back amongst his frozen companions, moving through time at an incredibly slow rate. Of course he gets back before the last commercial. I hope I do too.

Work

Through all of this, it is actually quite comforting to go to work. When I initially tell people, their first reaction is to ask me if I am going to take time off. I always tell them that work is one of the few things keeping me sane at this point. I mean, while teaching is not like plumbing or something where you can say, you know, I put these pipes in and now it works, I still have much more of an illusion of control at work than I do at home. At home I always have to face what's happening, and at work I don't.

Not to mention the fact that Kirsten is on my health insurance, and we don't have any kind of disability plan or family leave policy except for, you know, tons of unpaid time off, whoop-de-do. This is one of the downsides of the otherwise good experience of working in a charter school.

I had told my colleague Lisa about Kirsten's cancer immediately, and I end up telling the other people who have their desks in our big, windowless basement room, but that's only five of the thirty people who work here. So some people know and some people don't, and while I tell everybody it's not really a secret, I guess they feel awkward telling people, and so pretty soon I don't know who knows and who doesn't, and I get very tired of telling the whole story over and over. I have now taken to being kind of honest when people ask me polite questions like, "How's it going?" and replying with, "Incredibly shitty," and suchlike things. I know that is an incredibly annoying trait, but there you go.

On Thursday after our meeting with Maryann but before our meeting with Dr. J, I have a department meeting, and at the end of it I cry and cry and cry, and the nice women I work with ask what they can do, and since tomorrow is a professional development day, I ask if we can have our meeting off-site, with alcohol. They agree that that would be a good idea.

Friday morning I am still reeling from our meeting with Dr. J, and for some reason the worst part for me is that this treatment is going to kill Kirsten's ability to make blood. When I come in in the morning I end up telling somebody about this, and it just unhinges me to have to say that it's going to kill her blood. I don't know why—there are certainly other aspects that are just as horrible, but the thought of her getting medicine strong enough to kill her blood cells just makes me sad.

Somehow I drag my ass through this day, but it's not easy. When I am teaching, I usually have no trouble getting through the day—there are papers to be read, poems to be discussed, and many mini-crises to be dealt with. But on a professional development day, there are no kids in the building, and, though there is work to do, there is a lot more time to think. This is bad. I get through the morning, and after lunch I am shot—just too sad to do anything.

I decide to send an e-mail to everybody in the building basically explaining what's going on so that everybody knows and I don't have to have the initial conversation anymore. Here it is.

FROM: BRENDAN HALPIN
TO: STAFF
SUBJECT: MY LIFE

DISCLAIMER:
DEPRESSING PERSONAL
INFORMATION FOLLOWS.
FEEL FREE TO SKIP IT.

Many of you know some of this already, but here is the update. I am sorry to do this in an e-mail, but I am getting kinda worn out from having the conversation so many times.

My wife, Kirsten, has stage four breast cancer. (It has taken up residence on her spine.) After tons of tests, etc., we were faced with two treatment options. Option 1 involves getting chemo at standard doses pretty much continuously until death or until some promising new drug comes along, whichever comes first. Three guesses as to which one usually comes first. (Eighteen months to three years would be her projected survival under this plan. The oncologists say, "The intent of the treatment is not curative.")

The second plan involves basically three rounds of chemo. Round one is a pretty normal dose. The purpose of this is to bring stem cells from her bone marrow into her blood so they can be sucked out and stuck in the fridge. They become important later.

Round two involves three drugs given at ten times the standard dose. This involves a month-long hospitalization and tons of side effects, two of which are that her immune system and ability to make blood at all will be destroyed. Her own stem cells will be reinjected (they call this a transplant) and she will receive transfusions.

After three weeks at home, round three begins. This lasts twenty-one days and is given in the hospital on a semi-outpatient basis. That is to say, she will go to the hospital every day for treatment and stay if she, for example, spikes a fever. Most people are hospitalized about five days under this part of the treatment. She gets more of her stem cells at the end of this part.

And then, hopefully, that's it. Sixty percent of patients get a complete remission from this treatment. This can be a short- or long-lasting remission. The longest surviving patient from this study has been disease-free for eight years following the treatment.

Naturally I believe that my wife will be the exceptional person who achieves a permanent victory over this disease. It is a real bummer, though, to realize that given the current state of treatment for this disease, having her for only another ten years would be considered sort of miraculous. But there are exceptional people out there living cancer-free for a long time, and I think she will be one of them.

Frequently asked questions:

How are you holding up?

We are doing I guess about as well as can be expected. We are both very sad and angry that this is happening. I mean, Keith Richards is walking around relatively healthy and pushing sixty. Where's the justice? I need to be very strong and positive at home, so I may be pretty weak and feeble here. I am going to shave my head in a gesture of solidarity, so be prepared for me to look even more ridiculous in the next few weeks.

What can I do?

Many of you have already been very helpful and supportive. I appreciate your listening and checking in. Right now I feel very strongly that I need to continue working as much as I can. When I am teaching is about the only time that this situation is not foremost in my mind, and being relatively competent in the classroom gives me the illusion that some aspect of my life, at least, is under control.

Prayers, if you are so inclined, are helpful and appreciated.

If your religion and medical status permit it, a really con-
crete thing people can do is to donate blood and platelets.
Blood can't be earmarked for an individual patient, but
Kirsten will be needing a lot, and I feel, karmically speaking, that adding blood to the supply is a good and noble
way to honor her fight against this disease.

A platelet donation is a more time-consuming process (I
think it's a couple of hours vs. thirty minutes). I have no
idea if platelets can be donated in someone's name but I do
know that platelets donated at Jewish/Methodist Hospital
may well find their way to a woman undergoing the same
treatment, or to a leukemia or other patient undergoing
bone marrow or stem cell transplants.

Please feel free to ask me about stuff—I appreciate the affection and concern behind it, and I will certainly tell you if I
don't feel like talking about it. Please also feel free to not ask
me about it—I know many of you have difficult stuff happening in your life too or don't know me well enough to
watch me sob. I still like talking about sports, movies, and
teaching and appreciate opportunities to convince people that
Evil Dead 2 is the greatest movie of the twentieth century.

How's your daughter?

Okay so far. We are being honest and age-appropriate with her, and she is taking it well. The tough part will be the hospitalization, because our daughter (and all her under-six playmates) will be barred from visiting because kids are lil' germ factories who really shouldn't be hanging around with people with no immune systems. We'll see. The idea is to lose mom for a month in hopes of having her for many years.

What positive things are sustaining you?

We are surrounded by wonderful, loving family and friends. We feel loved, supported, and, most importantly, not alone. I feel blessed to have my wife, my child, a house of my own, and a job I love. I am happy to work with so many wonderful people. Thanks for listening.

—BH

Writing it feels kind of cathartic, and I sit and wait for the responses to roll in. I only get a couple on Friday, and the rest come on Monday. They range from expressions of concern and promises to pray to people telling me I'm brave and/or heroic, and one guy, who is not a native English speaker, adds that he thinks *Evil Dead 2* is "an adorable film." Not the first word that came to my mind when I watched it recently and guffawed as the disembodied head bites the crotch (I know I've mentioned it twice—it's really really funny), but I guess I do adore the movie.

I sure don't feel heroic, though. Or even brave. People will tell me this kind of stuff a lot, and I know they mean well, but I just think, well, what are my options here? How else can I be? I don't feel brave—I'm terrified. I don't feel like anybody's hero—I just get up and come to work every day, it's not like I risk my life saving Rwandan babies from genocide or anything. People think it takes extraordinary courage to live through something like this, but I guess I don't feel that way. What else can you do but get up every day and try to live your life? If I knew of an easier path, I would take it in a second.

After I write the e-mail and read a couple of replies, my department and I head off-site for our "meeting." It turns out to suck hard-core because I am just too too sad, and you know how alcohol is a great cure for sadness. I have also eaten a lot of cookies, and I feel kind of disgusting. I order a margarita, which is a mistake, because margaritas frequently major in sugar and minor in tequila and taste like vile Slurpees. This one appears to have failed tequila altogether, and I don't finish it. I start to cry after a while. Not because of anything in the conversation, but just because I am sad. My friends are very kind, and I know how much it sucks to hang out with somebody who is losing it, and this is a kindness I will remember for a long time. I finally say, "I just don't feel like I will ever feel any happiness or joy again." I can't imagine how I am going to live my life like this. It's unthinkable. I guess this is why people say I am courageous—because they can't imagine it either, and I have to do it.

The Hose

It is time for Kirsten to get her hose put in. This is something Dr. J told us about. Basically they will be pumping so much stuff into her veins and removing so much blood that it is just easier for everybody to have this two-way hose hanging out of her instead of searching for a vein to jab an IV in every time. Her mom stays over so she can take Rowen to preschool in the morning, and Kirsten and I head over to the day surgery unit at the hospital.

Now, this particular hospital is the product of a recent merger, and one "campus" is the old Jewish hospital, and the other "campus" is the old Methodist hospital. And I do not presume to make any sorts of sweeping religious judgments by this, but everything on the Methodist side is just a little older and shabbier. The dingy MRI suite and subterranean cafeteria are on the Methodist side, while the gleaming oncology suite with the bird's-eye-view of bad field hockey games is on the Jewish side. Before you leap to the "Jews with money" conclusion that, if you're honest, you know is on the tip of your mind right now, I should tell you that the whole beautiful building that houses the oncology suite is currently up for sale and this hospital as a whole seems to be in financial trouble. Here's hoping they stay open long enough to cure Kirsten.

We get to the day surgery wing at the shabby Methodist campus. It is 6:30 in the morning. There are a couple of old people in the waiting room. And this waiting room makes the MRI suite look like the halls of Valhalla. First of all, it is about the size of a gas station men's room. While significantly cleaner than a gas station bathroom, it has significantly worse reading material. At least in a gas station bathroom you can usually read some witticisms about people rolling their shit in little balls, or a big marijuana leaf with "SMOKE POT" emblazoned on it, or times and numbers for rendezvous for furtive homosexual activity, but here there is nothing. They taunt us with an empty magazine rack. This fits the pattern I have noticed of the more serious places having worse reading material, but it worries me a little. We are not yet to the most serious phase of this treatment, and already we are at zero for reading material. I don't know what the negative side of the magazine graph looks like. Do you have to give the nurse a magazine in order to be allowed to wait in the most serious places? I guess we will find out.

The lucky thing is that we don't really have to sit there very long before they call Kirsten to the back. I go with her. The nurse is nice and says I can't stay, but she allows me to go back to the desk with Kirsten and kiss her goodbye. The nurse asks if I want to be called when the surgery is done, just for my peace of mind. I say yes, and she makes sure she has the correct number. I give Kirsten a hug and a kiss, and the nurse says, "We'll take good care of her."

"You'd better," I say. It is still early, so I decide to walk to work. It is only about a twenty-minute walk, which makes me rethink my whole trolley-taking path. I feel sad, and not just because I am listening to the Carter Family as I walk. This is just one more thing that makes it all seem real. Just as I am about to hit work, I come to this song called "I Never Will Marry," which is a really haunting tune with this chorus:

> *I never will marry*
> *Or be no man's wife*
> *I expect to live single*
> *All the days of my life.*
> *The shells in the ocean*
> *Shall be my deathbed*
> *The fish in deep water*
> *Swim over my head.*

Yes, it is another song about a jilted lover taking her life, and though "all the days of my life" doesn't really make a whole lot of sense in the context of someone about to throw herself in the sea, it nevertheless moves me to tears. I listen to it three times in a row.

While I am at work, Kirsten is put under conscious sedation (which I had when I had my wisdom teeth out, and which is a really wonderful high, and which I would be administering to myself nightly right about now if I could get my hands on those wonderful wonderful drugs) and this hose is implanted in her chest wall. The hose has this mesh collar that is designed so her tissue will grow into it and really anchor it in there. This becomes important later.

By now it shouldn't surprise me, though it kind of does, that the jackasses never call me when the surgery is done. I check my voice mail kind of frantically all day and finally decide that while they don't give a shit about my peace of mind, they probably would have called if she had died on the table. But why the hell did they say they would call?

Hosed

The hose is problematic immediately. First and most important, it is very painful to Kirsten, and it pretty much disables her. She can't reach over her head, which means she has a very hard time getting dressed, and she's not allowed to lift anything, which Rowen takes kind of personally, and which, overall, puts a lot of limits on what you can do. We can't, for example, really hug her anymore. We can sort of gingerly place our arms around her while she winces and goes, "Watch out for the hose!" but that's not really the same.

Also, psychologically it is tough. Up to now, Kirsten, except for having a fatal disease waiting to take over her whole body, has not been sick at all. She is now pretty obviously in pain and unable to do things she used to do, and I get this "Oh shit, here we go" feeling.

She is supposed to have these visiting nurses come out to tell her how to flush out the lines and everything, or possibly to do it for her, and there is some kind of colossal mix-up on the first day, but the nurse eventually arrives and gives Kirsten a five-minute and terribly confusing tutorial on how to draw some blood out, pump this anticoagulant in, and keep it all fine and dandy. Kirsten is game, but soon one of the lines is filled with blood, and this isn't supposed to happen, and this is on a

Saturday, so she calls Dr. J, and Dr. J gets another visiting nurse to come out, and this visiting nurse is male, which does sort of disconcert her at first, but he turns out to be much kinder and more helpful than the first nurse. He is patient and professional and explains things clearly and in detail, and he flushes out the hose.

Kirsten gets her initial doses of chemo through the hose, and then, a few days later, it fills with blood again. She goes back to the hospital, and they determine that the hose is actually broken, and they apparently root around the back room looking for parts so they can fix it and find that the parts are on order from Korea or the Philippines or wherever they pay some kid twenty cents a day to put this piece of shit together, so they have to remove it. Kirsten is in the hands of the day surgery people, so Dr. J is not actually there, and apparently the doctor, whose name I have but guess I should not write since everybody else in this book gets a pseudonym, is a total asshole. "Well," he says to Kirsten in this annoyed tone, "I have another *scheduled* one in a few minutes, so I can do this now, but if you really want to have the *drugs,* you're going to have to come back *late late this afternoon,* and *maybe* we can *try* to *squeeze* you in . . ." You get the idea. This is one of these "choices" they give you that's really no choice at all, because you are already there, let's just get this over with, so they give her a shot of Lidocaine, which is I guess like novocaine—some kind of local anesthetic, and these are famously ineffective on Kirsten—she usually needs three times what the dentist thinks is a reasonable amount in order to really get numb, but clearly Dr. Mengele here is not really concerned about getting her numb, so he shoots her up and yanks the hose out, and you may recall that the hose is designed so that your tissue grows into it, and so it is incredibly painful, and Dr. Mengele is an asshole about it, and she is in pain and she is incredibly sad.

I find out all this when I get home that day, and I am ready to go down to the hospital and raise hell about Dr. Mengele, I can't believe they ripped this thing out of her with a shot of a crappy local anesthetic (and, later on, other medical professionals will also be incredulous), but Kirsten says there's really no point, it's not like he did anything wrong, he was just a dick. I think that *is* doing something wrong, but it's not the kind of thing that you usually get a lot of satisfaction complaining about.

Except complaining about it right now is pretty satisfying, and if there is any justice in this universe at all, which I have come to doubt pretty severely, this guy will at some point become a torture victim and I'll do a reverse Amnesty thing and write to his captors telling them to keep up the good work, and mail them car batteries and bamboo shoots and whatever else they need to keep this motherfucker in pain.

She Doesn't Want to Canoe

The last weekend before Kirsten starts her chemo is our anniversary weekend. We do not plan anything romantic, mostly because Kirsten has this hose dangling out of her and feels kind of crappy. We decide to head down to her parents' house. They live a block away from the beach, about an hour from here. We spent many weekends down there just before we moved, when we were afraid the Troll was really going to flip his lid and do something scary. We all got very comfortable down there, and it's a big enough house that we can be down there without everybody feeling like they are on top of each other, which is important.

So we all head down there and have a very nice, relaxing weekend. Sort of. The thing is, Kirsten's impending treatment is hanging over the whole weekend. What we want is just to head down there and hang out and forget everything, but Kirsten's parents seem to want to make this a special weekend for us, and while we appreciate the impulse, it does get kind of strange, and their desire to make it special keeps reminding us that it is special, that after this weekend all the shit starts. They decide at some point that we should take the canoe out and do some canoeing. I am game, but Kirsten seems kind of lukewarm. She says something like, "I don't know if I really feel like it," but apparently this is not sufficiently negative, because the next thing we know, the canoe is strapped to the top of Kirsten's mom's car, and her dad keeps saying things like "Hey, you guys ready to take the canoe out?"

Kirsten eventually has to bite her parents' heads off to make them understand that she doesn't want to canoe. I feel bad about this whole thing. We are both kind of depressed—we have just lived through the week with our epic meetings with Maryann and Dr. J, and I can totally see how her parents want to do something that will be special and fun, but they are being so solicitous that it keeps reminding us that this is not just a normal weekend, which is all we really wanted.

Still, it's nice to hang out. We go to playgrounds a lot, and I get my Rollerblades, which I have used about three times since

I bought them, out of the trunk and do some great skating on the traffic-free streets of this sleepy rich sailing town in the off-season. I also start writing this in a notebook that Kirsten's dad gives her. The sense that the shit is en route to the fan casts a pall over the whole weekend, though.

One notable thing happens when we are at this playground with Rowen, and we are playing this game where she drops me off on one play structure and says, "Okay. You have a good day at school, honey, I have to go to work now," and then runs over to another play structure for a minute, then comes back and "picks me up" so we can go to our "home," which is a third play structure. So there I am enjoying my day at "school" when I see this very attractive woman jog up with her jogging stroller and toddler, and I am kind of admiring the whole look—you know, attractive young mom all sweaty and spandex-clad—and about five minutes later her much older husband comes wheezing up to the playground. He is also decked out in jogging gear, but his wife was pushing a stroller and beat him by a solid five minutes.

I immediately judge the guy, which I am sure I will pay for eventually, and I am seized by a desire to kick him to death. I mean, when a guy in his fifties shows up with his twenty-years-younger wife and toddler, you just know there's a fifty-something ex-wife and kids just barely younger than the trophy wife somewhere. Right? I mean, I am sure there are exceptions, but this is the rule.

And I just get so mad at this guy. Now again, I don't know his specific situation—maybe his first wife was an abusive drug addict or something, or maybe he's even widowed—but I can't help feeling that he has a perfectly good wife somewhere that he threw away because she got old. And all I want is for my wife to get old.

The Mice

When we moved into our new house, it became clear that it was infested with mice. We have baseboard heat, and under all of the radiators were lines of turds. Behind the oven and washing machines was the telltale blue-green of mouse poison and, of course, a ton of turds.

We occasionally see the mice running through the halls at night, and I always find turds on my stove and countertops in the morning. I love to cook, and therefore do basically all the cooking. I like it because it is creative—take a bunch of stuff and mix it together to make something wonderful—and it's finite. You chop some stuff up, you cook it, and you eat it. Done. This is incredibly unlike teaching, where nothing is ever complete. You do get kids coming back years later and saying you changed their lives, which rarely happens after you've cooked even a really fantastic meal, but you very very rarely feel at the end of the day or even the end of the year like what you wanted to do is done. There's always more to do. This is not the case with cooking.

So cooking is very therapeutic for me, and I take it kind of personally when mice shit in my frying pan. Or on my countertops, or all over my industrial-size can of sesame oil that I made a special trip to the Chinese market for. So when we first move in, I buy a bunch of poison and scatter it throughout the house. Of course, it doesn't work at all. This is probably more a comment on our housekeeping than anything else. I mean, if you are a mouse, are you going to go for poison or for some succulent crumbs of last night's dinner that are here, there, or everywhere? It's really no contest.

I am doubly concerned because this is a three-family house, and as landlords we have a legal obligation to keep the building vermin-free, which is easier said than done. So I go for the glue traps. It has been my experience in the past that the flip traps don't work at all, so I buy the glue traps even though I have a very traumatic memory of catching a mouse in a glue trap when I was about ten years old and flipping this screaming mouse into a bucket of water. It was horrifying.

But I'm not ten years old anymore, so I figure I can deal with it. At first it looks like it's not even going to be an issue because they studiously ignore the glue traps. One mouse even manages to shit in a glue trap without getting stuck. I am convinced this is the mousy way of saying "fuck you."

But I stick with it because nothing else is working, and one night I hear a loud squeee squeee squeee, and I see a mouse caught in the trap I have wedged between the garbage and the countertop. I will come to call this "the money spot," because while the mice will continue to ignore every other trap in all of their favorite locations, I will catch at least six more in traps put in this exact spot.

When I hear this squee squee squee, I put my plan into action. I go to the rag bag and grab a rag, which I place over the mouse. I then go to the bookshelf and grab the giant hardcover French-English dictionary I have had since high school. I hear the voice of my ninth-grade French teacher echoing in my head, going, "People, spend the extra money for the hardcover dictionary! You'll be glad you did!"

I drop the dictionary on the mouse, and boom—he's gone. I pop the rag-covered corpse in the trash, and I'm done. I feel like I should seek out Monsieur Stirling and tell him, but I guess this probably isn't the use he had in mind.

At first this is kind of fun. I feel good about giving the mice a more humane death than they get from poison, and I feel good about getting some revenge for that shit in my frying pan. It does not bother me at all.

And then Kirsten is diagnosed, and the news just keeps getting worse and worse and worse. And suddenly I feel kind of bad for doling out death, especially when we are trying like hell to fight against Kirsten's. It seems like bad karma. But what the hell am I going to do? They can't stay here, and while you can ask them to leave, they don't usually comply. So I have to kill them. But I start to hate it. What makes me incredibly sad is that they stop screaming before I drop the dictionary on them. They stop screaming as soon as they are covered in the rag. Does it comfort them to be covered up? Or do they know that it's pointless to scream because their situation has just gotten hopeless?

Chemo Begins

Kirsten starts her chemo on a Monday. I spend the day on a bus, on some incredibly ill-advised trip with my school to try to climb a mountain in the rain. On the way up, one of the science teachers makes us watch *October Sky,* about which they say, "It's great! It's about science!" I guess this is why only science teachers went to see it, but I watch it because it's on, and it turns out to be pretty engrossing, except for the fact that Laura Dern, who I have had a crush on since *Blue Velvet* in 1986, dies of lymphoma in this movie. Great. Perfect fucking thing to watch while your wife is starting chemo for her stage four breast cancer. I pretend to be interested in the scenery or the bus driver's ranting about how if he were in the lead bus, he would have taken a different route (the guys who drive charter buses are a weird, weird bunch), so that I don't start sobbing.

I have my cell phone with me. (Yes, I did eventually get one because I was freaking out over the idea of Kirsten being in the hospital and me not being able to go to the grocery store, but also because it felt like I was doing something, which of course I wasn't.) We are out of the service area up here on the mountain, so I have to wait till the bus ride home to call her. She is shockingly upbeat. She says the whole thing took less than half an hour, and she feels fine.

The chemo was a comparative breeze. And it will be the next two days too. The famous nausea never makes an appearance, and she still has all her hair.

After a few days, she gets tired. Really tired. Not exactly can't-get-off-the-couch kind of tired, but definitely can't-take-a-fifteen-minute-walk kind of tired. This is kind of a drag, but it is really not that bad—I have seen her this bad before when she's had the flu or a cold. It is no fun, but it is not an "Oh my God she's so sick the cure is as bad as the disease" kind of thing.

God Intervenes After All

As the news of Kirsten's illness spreads, the notes start pouring in. I get an especially large number of cards and letters (and even some rather generous checks) from my relatives in Cincinnati, who are a group of people I like but have never been especially close to. (This is because my mom was the only one out of seven kids to become anything close to a hippie, and she was not incredibly tight with her family while I was growing up. Now she's back in the fold and I'm eight hundred miles away.) They call and write to let me know that we are in their prayers.

My friends are also calling and writing to check in. Basically everyone we know with a child Rowen's age offers to help out by taking care of her. My friend Karl comes to visit and burns me a couple of CDs of Johnny Cash songs I don't already own. Kirsten's sister, Nan, comes to visit and does our laundry and cleaning for a week, in addition to providing valuable moral support and baby-sitting while Kirsten and I go see *The Legend of Drunken Master,* which is one of only a handful of sequels better than the original. (The others: *Evil Dead 2, The Texas Chainsaw Massacre 2, Superman II, Batman Returns*—I know what you're thinking about *The Godfather, Part II,* but I still like the first one better.)

Kirsten's mom and dad are up here all the time working on our house and taking Kirsten to appointments or taking Rowen to school. Friends take me out for beers. Lisa tells me that she has been talking to lots of people at work who want to help in some way.

And Carol Bell (which is not a pseudonym) coordinates this whole thing at our church where people come to our house every week to clean, and we have a list of people to call in the middle of the night in case of an emergency. I mean, people come to our house every Saturday and clean our toilet just because they want so much to be doing something for us.

It is very difficult under such circumstances to maintain the idea that God is not working in the world. When we are in our time of need, we are suddenly surrounded by love and we can't forget even for a day how many people care about us.

In one of those coincidences that also sometimes make me faithful, somebody at church mentions, by way of saying something else, that Saint Teresa of Avila said, "God has no hands but our hands." If that's true, what a stupid ingrate I've been to suggest that God is not working in the world.

A Tough Time for Him Too

As I said at the beginning, husbands usually get a sentence or two in the cancer literature. There is a husbands-of-cancer-patients support group at the hospital, but I frankly feel like I'd want to throttle anybody who was fifty and worried about losing his wife. I know that's uncharitable, but given what they are telling us now, it will be a miracle if Kirsten lives to be fifty. I believe in this miracle—I have to. But I am also keenly aware of the odds. So I'd kind of want to slap these guys and tell them to shut the fuck up and be happy about the eighteen extra years they got of having a wife without cancer that I will never have. Assholes.

Plus, really, the idea of trying to carve out time to sit around and cry with random old men just stresses me out more. Where exactly is the time supposed to come from?

So here is what "a tough time for him" means to me now. I am typing this at 5:43 A.M. I got up at 5:23 A.M. I went to bed at 10:07 P.M. I then woke up at 2:36 A.M. This is pretty good. For the last week I have been waking up every two hours, so the fact that I got four and a half is pretty spectacular. I lie awake for an indeterminate amount of time. This is not really surprising or unusual. After lying awake for some time, I fall back asleep. At 4:03 A.M. Rowen is screaming that she has to pee. She is not yet four, so this means that I have to get up and take her to the bathroom while she cries and is crabby about being awake. She yells that her pee won't stop coming, and I have to admit that it is pretty spectacular—it lasts for about a full minute, and I think we are very lucky that she was able to hold it. And then she yells that she doesn't want to wipe, after which she yells at me for wiping the wrong way. She goes back to sleep. I, of course, lie awake for another indeterminate amount of time.

At 5:13, she screams, "I'm scared! I'm scared!" Kirsten, half asleep, says, "She's peeing."

"No way," I reply, "she just peed a river about an hour ago!"

"Well, go see what's wrong!" Kirsten says in an annoyed voice. So I stumble out of bed again, and into Rowen's room. She tells me that she's afraid of monsters. I give her a hug and tell her there are no monsters. She says that she needs to sleep somewhere else. Three guesses where that is.

I go back to bed and tell Kirsten that Rowen wants to sleep with us. Right after this, Rowen starts yelling about how she wants to sleep with us. People who are willing to yell to get their way in the middle of the night usually get their way so everybody can sleep. At least that's the case in this house. I mean, she would yell and cry for an hour, or we can just let her in the bed and at least two of us can get back to sleep. So that's what happens. Rowen climbs into bed at 5:23. I just get up, because I have to be up at 6:00 anyway, and I know I won't get back to sleep. So I sit here while Kirsten and Rowen sleep. They will both get right back to sleep and probably sleep until at least 7:00.

I will leave the house at 6:45. I will be expected to be patient, civil, and competent with teenage advisees at 7:30. I also have to make a presentation to my department today at 8:30.

So I feel petulant and resentful. I have to take care of Kirsten because, you know, well, she has cancer, and I have to take care of Rowen because, you know, well, she's not quite four years old, and that all makes sense, but who's taking care of me? Who cares that I got less than five hours of sleep and I have to go work a full day? Who gives me a hug when I feel scared in the middle of the night? I can't even tell anybody I feel scared because it's my job to be positive.

So I will go and put in a nine-hour day on five hours of sleep. During this time I will worry constantly about whether Kirsten is okay and whether she can reach me if she needs to. I will probably call home to check in two or three times. Did I mention that I also need to be competent at my job?

The really great part about all this is that I also feel guilty about feeling petulant and resentful. I am not four and I don't have cancer.

It's a tough time for him too.

The Troll. Again.

So I am getting on the subway to pick Rowen up at preschool one day, and the car is crowded, but I do see an empty seat, so I start to make for it when I realize it is right next to Mrs. Troll. I turn around and decide to stand. I find my heart pumping and my fists clenching as I imagine all the great stuff I could say to her if she started with me. I am surprised to find how angry I still am about everything that happened with them. When it gets to be Mrs. Troll's stop, she gets up and has to pass within about an inch of me. I know she sees me because she kind of does a little stutter-step but then keeps walking out smoothly. We used to see each other on the subway from time to time when we were locked in battle over Rowen walking, and we got pretty good at ignoring each other. You know, writing it down and looking at it, it looks completely absurd. I really can't believe I spent three years of my life trying to work out a conflict with the kind of people who think their rights are being violated by a kid walking. I kind of regret that I didn't smile or blow her a kiss, but what can you do.

I go to pick up Rowen and I meet Kirsten there. I am still practically shaking with anger. I eventually figure out why I am so angry. It's because the script didn't go the way I planned. We were supposed to leave our old house and move and be happy, leaving the Troll to stew in his own juices of hate and resentment. And what happened was we moved and were happy and then found out that Kirsten has a potentially fatal illness. And I'm the one who's hateful and resentful. How is it that we, who tried to seek a peaceful solution to our conflict, who tried to accommodate their lunacy by buying rugs, we who are not assholes (well, at least Kirsten's not), are suffering, while they are not?

And then I think, well, would I want to be him? Would I, even now, trade places with him? No way. Cobbling together a living, doing whatever folk singers do to make money, he mostly sits in a dark room in his basement and makes angry phone calls and sends angry letters, faxes, and e-mails. I would not be him for anything, even a healthy wife. Life, even with a healthy wife, seems to involve a lot of suffering for him all the time. And right now, even in the midst of everything, I am thankful every day to live in this house instead of above the Troll. Rowen will shriek or stomp or something, and I will remember the gut-wrenching anxiety I used to feel every time that happened in the old house, and I will be happy I don't live there.

The irony is that while we bought this house and figured that people who didn't like the noise of kids basically didn't have to be our tenants, this house is practically soundproof. The other irony is that the Troll always wanted us to get wall-to-wall carpets (though I am sure that wouldn't have helped, since the rugs didn't) and we sort of drew the line at spending thousands of dollars to accommodate his lunacy, and then we went and bought a house with wall-to-wall carpets. Go figure.

Speaking of his angry e-mails, I get one about two days after

I see his wife on the subway. It has to do with my trusteeship in the condo association, which I resigned when we closed, but which our lawyer evidently forgot to send to the association. Our lawyer, surprisingly enough, has not been returning calls from a long-winded blowhard he doesn't work for, so now the Troll wants me to get involved. Of course, what it is really about is having the last word. During the days before we moved, we had the police out to have a lengthy talk with him, basically telling him that his rights were not being violated, we were moving anyway, and he needed to back off. This seemed to scare him off communicating with us directly until we moved. He sent everything to our lawyer. But now that the dust has settled, he can't resist berating me for leaving some stuff in the basement (I think I have done this everywhere I have ever lived that had a basement). He says I am "a weird kid."

This just about knocks me out. I am getting through my days pretty well, and, for the most part, I have the energy to get through the day, do my job, and communicate with everybody in a pretty good way, but after getting this e-mail, I just want to go straight to bed. I just have no energy for anything extra right now. I can handle all the regular stuff, but when something unexpected comes up, I do not have any gas in the reserve tank.

I call our lawyer and get this straightened out. I am in no way above milking my situation to get better service, so I say, "Look, Kirsten has breast cancer, and the last thing I want to be dealing with right now is this asshole." He takes care of it.

I do take some comfort from the fact that the e-mail seems to reveal that he doesn't know Kirsten is sick. This comforts me, because several people on our old street know, and it wouldn't surprise me at all if it got back to him. And he is the only person in the world I don't want to know, because I know it would make him glad.

I spend a couple of days composing replies about how rich it is to be called weird by a guy I've seen yelling obscenities and chucking his dinner across the backyard, about how ironic it is to be called a kid by a childless musician who thinks he has a lot of responsibility because he swears at contractors a lot, but eventually I realize that what he really wants is for me to get into this with him again. I sort of want that too, but I realize it would be pointless. He is never ever going to read a put-down from me and go, "By gum, he is correct! I've been an abominable cad!" So if I can't convince him, what's the point? There is no point. I add his address to the "blocked senders" list, and it feels pretty good.

Fever

Kirsten's counts are low. I'm not exactly sure which counts we are talking about here—white blood cells? T cells?—but anyway, they say that about a week after you get chemo, your counts get low. This is because the chemo kills the cells in the pipeline, so to speak, rather than the ones already in your blood, so when you are ready for this week's infusion of white blood cells, you find yourself a little short.

She is under explicit instructions to keep an eye on her temperature, and if she runs a fever of 101, to quote Dr. J, "that's an automatic overnight in the hospital." It is Saturday, and Nan is here, and the two of them are consuming just awe-inspiring amounts of chocolate, and Kirsten feels a little hot, so she begins taking her temperature obsessively. She has the thermometer in her mouth like every twenty minutes. I have a feeling that we are definitely headed to the hospital soon.

I am right. Her temperature creeps up as the day goes on, and late in the afternoon she announces, "One oh one point five." I page the doctor on call and get no response, so I hang up and page her again, and she eventually calls and says yes, go to the emergency room, and I think, great, emergency room on Saturday night—we'll have to sit there for hours while they process the car wrecks and gunshot wounds. I am freaking out, because she is going to have to spend the night in the hospital, and this reminds me that soon she'll have to spend three weeks in the hospital, but mostly it just sucks because we were having a really nice, relaxing Saturday at home, and now here's cancer again, reminding us that we don't have a normal life. I am also kind of freaked out because, you know, she has this compromised immune system, and she has a fever.

Nan is also freaking out, but Kirsten is shockingly calm. In fact, when I drop her off at the emergency room on the way to park in the garage, she says, "Okay, well, I guess I'll call you when they get me into a room," and I have to explain that no, we are just going to the parking garage, we're not going to just drop her off in the emergency room, and she says, "Oh, okay, but, you know, don't feel like you have to. This is really no big deal. Dr. J said this happens to everybody." She means this, and I know she's right because I was there when Dr. J said this, but it doesn't make it seem any easier.

We wait in the waiting room, and I look around at all the sad and depressed faces. It's tough to tell who the sick ones are. Everybody looks tired and morose. One guy sitting near us was, I overheard the security guard saying, lying on the bathroom floor a few minutes ago. Now he is slumped across two seats and occasionally lifts his head to cough or sneeze, and after we sit there for forty-five minutes or so, I think, well, this is just a great place for someone with a compromised immune system to be hanging out. I mean, there must be a better way for them to do this than to have us sit in the emergency waiting room, which is probably one of the most septic places in the city, for close to an hour, inhaling God knows what kind of Ebola viruses people are spewing out.

Despite my annoyance and anxiety, I sit there incessantly singing the only two lines of "Fever" I know until Kirsten finally snaps, as she usually does when I sing the same bit of song over and over, which is almost daily: "Hon, either sing some more lines of that song or pick another song."

"But it's 'Fever,' " I protest. "Get it?"

"I don't know that song. Nan, do you know that song?" She doesn't. The joke is lost, so I stop, which is just as well. I was starting to annoy even myself.

Eventually they take Kirsten toward the back, and I want to go with her just to basically say goodbye, though she really doesn't seem to care one way or the other, and as I leave, Rowen is clinging to me, tears streaming down her face, saying, "Daddy! Don't go!" and I try to explain that I'll only be gone a minute, and she can sit with Aunty Nan, but she is past listening, so I just wrench her fingers away, and I go back to the emergency room, and Kirsten has disappeared. In the ten seconds it took me to pry myself away, she is gone.

I finally have to ask to find her, and I go in and kiss her good-bye, and I'm feeling all morose, and she is totally upbeat. "I'll call you! See you in the morning!"

When we get home, Rowen falls asleep instantly, and I cook dinner and open a bottle of wine. Nan and I have just started eating, and my glass is about half empty, when the phone rings. It's Kirsten. "I'm coming home!" she says. I am annoyed that once again we have been told something categorically ("automatic overnight") that turns out to be not so categorical, but mostly I am just happy she's coming home and I get to sleep next to her tonight.

What Love Is

"My hair is falling out in clumps," Kirsten tells me on the phone when I call from work. "We're shaving tonight."

I am delighted. My hair has been getting big again. Though I have straight hair, it does not really get long—it just gets big, like Adam Rich from *Eight Is Enough*. It has been getting big for a while now, but I have resisted going down to Sal's barber shop because I figure why spend twelve bucks on a haircut when I am going to shave off all my hair soon anyway.

When I get home it is difficult for me to look at the pile of hair Kirsten has on her lap. She has been sitting on the couch obsessively pulling at her hair, and she has now gathered together a ferret-sized pile.

I have to go to Kmart to buy some clippers, so I head over there after Rowen goes to bed. It is a miserable fall night, about 40 degrees and rainy, the kind of weather that has always pissed me off—I figure if it's that cold, it should be snowing. U2's new song, "Beautiful Day," seems to be playing on every station. I love this song. It is about the only noncountry song that has really spoken to me since this whole thing started, and while, you know, it ain't "The Long Black Veil," Bono's melancholy insistence that it's a beautiful day just about mirrors my state of mind as I drive through cold rain to buy clippers to shave my wife's head.

I find the clippers quickly. Well, what I actually find is a twenty-four-piece hair-cutting kit with instructional video *How to Cut Hair at Home* in English and español. (I guess it's something like *Como Cortar el Pelo en la Casa* in Spanish, but I don't really know because I took French in high school.)

I sneak over to Toys "R" Us after buying the clippers and look longingly at the video game systems. I do not now own nor have I ever owned a video game system, but I am in the grips of another fit of "Buy my way out of this" fever, and my current obsession is video games, because TV sucks really bad and I don't really ever have the energy to read or do much of anything creative except write, and I can only really do that when I am feeling shitty. I look at all the systems, then decide I can't do it tonight because Kirsten would totally kill me. Whenever I have mentioned getting a PlayStation or something in an even half-joking way, she has absolutely forbidden it, and right now while she is losing her hair, feeling like shit, and has a hose sticking out of her neck is not the greatest time for me to start defying her wishes. Plus, there is just something creepy and depressing about Toys "R" Us. Maybe it's all the crying kids. Maybe it's the harried-looking adults. Whatever it is, it feels like a desperate place, and buying anything there would feel like a desperate act, so I run back in the cold rain to my car and my clippers.

I get home and attack Kirsten's head with the clippers. I have never used them before, so I fit them with the biggest attachment and start trying to cut through Kirsten's hair. The clippers keep getting clogged, and when that happens, I have to sort of tug them out, which pulls on the hair still attached to Kirsten's head, causing her to say "Ow!" on top of being very tired and cranky already. So I start with scissors. I indiscriminately hack off her hair until it is close to pixie length. Then back to the clippers. Now they are working much better, and we progress through the attachments until we reach one eighth of an inch. It's like mowing the lawn—the clippers just sail over her head, buzzing it down to stubble. This is kind of satisfying, but it also makes me kind of sad to see all her hair on the floor. She can't move very well because of the hose sticking out of her neck, and it really feels like I am removing the last brick from the wall of denial that has served us so well. Up to now she has been feeling bad, but mostly just tired, and she has looked basically normal but for the various hoses sticking out of her. Now she has patchy tennis ball fuzz. Soon she'll be completely bald. Miraculously, I manage to focus on the satisfaction of a job well done and I do not cry. Perhaps even more miraculously, Nan, who is watching the whole affair and who I was convinced was going to start bawling, does not.

I keep finding myself thinking, You don't know what love is till you shave your wife bald. Of course that's not really true, but it also is. I meant it when I said for better or for worse, in sickness and in health, but I kind of thought that meant, you know, we wouldn't have any money for a while, I'd buy her lozenges when she had a cold, and then listen to her complain about her arthritis when she was eighty. I never really thought it meant shaving her head while she fights for her life at age thirty-two.

When we are done with Kirsten, we start on me. I attack my own head with the scissors, then Kirsten and I go after my hair with the clippers. I go beyond the eighth-of-an-inch attachment to no attachment at all, which cuts me down to one sixteenth of an inch. I then head to the bathroom, lather up my head and shave it with my Gillette Sensor. I am surprised to find that my scalp is much less sensitive than my cheeks and neck, and except for the fact that it's kind of tough to tell when you miss a spot in the back, it's really not that bad to shave your head with a razor.

We settle into bed that night, and Kirsten is sort of in agony from the hose sticking out of her neck. She lies down and I have to pull her up because it hurts too much to use the muscles in her neck to pull herself up. So I yank her up a few times, give her my pillow to prop her up more, and feel sad while she goes "Ouch!" rustle, turn, "Shit!" rustle, turn, "God! Damn!" rustle, turn for about five minutes till she finds a position she can sleep in.

For all this, I feel good. It feels like we've done something.

My First Day Bald

I walk to work with my fleece hat on, and see a few kids on the way in, and reluctantly take my hat off. I feel kind of awkward, knowing I am going to have to spend the day explaining, but also because it's fucking cold when you have no hair, especially in New England in the fall and winter. I am sitting in my house typing this right now and it is in the high 30s outside, and our house is pretty cozy, but my head is ridiculously cold. I need a hat before I can continue.

Anyway, I take off my hat and I know the kids are going to make fun of me, and they do not disappoint. One kid who was my student last year goes into paroxysms of laughter, rubs my head, and laughs that "it's not even smooth!" It's true. My head is stubbly. Although I shave my face every day, I have never really needed to, whereas people like my friend Danny look like they need a shave about thirty seconds after they shave, and I now have some sympathy with them, because that's pretty much what my head is like.

One wacky aspect of having a stubbly head that it takes me weeks to get used to is the effect I call "Velcro head." It is now basically impossible to slip a shirt or sweater off or on and have it slide effortlessly over my head. The stubble just Velcros it right in place, and I have to reach in and lift it off my head or it just stays there.

My advisees know that Kirsten has cancer, as do my classes, so they are kind of prepped. I had kind of hoped that they would tell everybody else, but there seems to be something about genuine tragedy that stops the rumor mill cold. I will explain to probably ten students why I have shaved my head before school even starts, and yet I have to keep explaining all day long. All I can think is that whenever somebody looks at someone else's boyfriend the wrong way, or calls someone else a bitch or whatever, the entire school knows about it in like thirty seconds, they sometimes seem to know about it before it happens, but the kids are just not spreading the word around. I can't figure it out. I like to interpret it in a touching way—like maybe they are just too respectful of the situation to turn it into gossip. Or maybe they just can't stand to talk about cancer because it scares the shit out of them. I understand. It scares the shit out of me too.

One kid in particular suffers from the breakdown of the rumor mill. In the midst of about five kids clowning me pretty severely, this one kid says, "Mr. Halpin, do you have cancer?" ha-ha-ha, and I say, "No, but my wife does," and he says, "You're joking, right?" and I say, "I wish I was," and the poor kid looks like I just kicked him in the teeth. I sympathize, because it's exactly the kind of dumb insensitive thing I would have said at his age and felt terrible. He is not my student, but he seeks me out later in the day to apologize, and I tell him that he should not even think about it, and I mean it, because I really have said worse things. The worst thing I ever said—well, let's just say I once made up a parody of Eric Clapton's "Tears in Heaven," because, you know, I was twenty-three, and I thought that his cranking out twenty years' worth of really mediocre music was this incredible crime that pretty much justified my saying any kind of horrible thing I could think of, and then I had a kid, and while I still don't like the song, I feel like a total asshole for making fun of the tragedy behind it. The only positive thing to come out of that is that I was quick to forgive the kid who made the cancer joke. In fact, it's wrong to even call it forgiveness, because not for a nanosecond was I offended. I felt bad for him the instant he said it.

So once people hear why I did it, they are all very supportive. The girls go, "Awwwwwwwww . . . ," and the boys kind of give me manly affirmation, and I feel okay about it all. For one thing, I turn out to have a really great-shaped head, and relatively small ears, so I don't look that ridiculous. For another thing, I kind of like wearing this marker of tragedy around. I seem to remember hearing that Buddhist monks and nuns shave their heads as a sign that they have renounced the world, or worldly things, or desire, or whatever exactly it is that they have renounced, and I feel the same way. I have felt different from everybody else for weeks now, and now I have this visible sign of my difference, and for some strange reason that feels good. It's not that I want pity or anything, though of course I do, but I just like feeling like I am wearing a sign that says, "I'm not like you."

On my way home after work I walk by the coffee shop across the street and spy no fewer than three young hipsters with heads shaved bald. I guess I should be glad that it's some sort of mini fashion trend, so not everyone will look at me like I'm a total freak when I walk down the street, but the thing is, I kind of want to be a total freak. I don't want anyone to think this is a fashion statement. Oh well. I don't want a lot of things these days.

The Roller Coaster

I think of my emotional life now as kind of a roller coaster, which is not incredibly accurate, because roller coasters are fun, especially the Beast at Kings Island in Ohio, which I grew up with. It's really great. You should ride it if you get the chance.

On the other hand, I recommend that you stay the hell away from the Spouse With Cancer ride. It is like a roller coaster in that there are ups and downs, and I have to be honest that there are still ups, and despite what I said to my co-workers, joy and fun have not abandoned me, but the downs are really really down. Subterranean.

The weird thing about this ride is that it has really long flat stretches. Not up, not down—just flat. Some days I feel happy and full of energy, and some days I feel like I'm about to cry all day, but most days I just feel numb. I guess this is really a down in disguise, but it doesn't feel bad. In fact it doesn't feel at all. It is just blank. I am usually able to muster up some enthusiasm at work, but then it becomes time to go home, and I just think about how I have five hours until I go to bed, and I am not feeling at all enthusiastic about anything that's going to happen between now and then. People ask me how I am on days like this and I say, "Alive."

I guess the flats are a defense mechanism to stop me from feeling down all the time, but it is so strange. I feel disconnected, like I am missing something. I know there are these intense feelings lurking around, but they don't surface. I know that I love my work, but I don't feel excited going in like I normally do. I love my family, but I don't feel happy about going home. I love food, but I don't get a thrill from eating. I hate cancer, I'm terrified of losing Kirsten, but I don't feel the fear. I'm just numb. I guess lots of people medicate themselves with excessive amounts of drugs or alcohol to try to achieve this state, so I probably shouldn't complain, but it just feels like my life is on hold right now. We will return to our regularly scheduled life as soon as we figure out whether your wife is going to live or die. But when will that be? Suppose we only have five years, or ten. I need to find a way to enjoy most of that time. Do I do that by just ignoring reality, or is there some way to live with this?

I guess this is really everybody's problem. How do you live knowing you could die at any time? I think for most of us we just pretty much deny the possibility that we are ever going to die. But once you face it, how do you ignore it again? Or can you become the kind of person who enjoys life *because* you know you're going to die?

I don't know the answers. Maybe I'll figure it out when I get off this ride.

Thich Nhat Hanh My Ass

It is a beautiful Friday afternoon three weeks after Kirsten's first chemo treatment. She has been feeling much better for a couple of days. Bald, yes, but more energetic and positive than she's been for weeks. I leave work a little earlier than usual and decide to walk home instead of taking the subway.

The sun is shining, I have had a good week at work, and I feel happy. I wonder if I am in denial again, and then I think maybe I am just getting to be some kind of Zen master. A few days earlier Carol from church, who is spearheading the cleanup effort, said to me on the phone that Thich Nhat Hanh, a Buddhist monk who is quoted quite frequently by people in our church, says that life is almost always bearable moment to moment—that it is anticipating and remembering that are really painful.

I have read some Thich Nhat Hanh and have always felt that he basically holds the key to happiness, and that I could achieve it if I weren't so lazy. Basically he's all about living in the moment—being constantly grateful for your life, aware that you are alive and enjoying just the wonderfulness of breathing. I really do believe that this is the key to being happy. There is only one problem: it's really really hard.

In order to get to a place where you can believe this deep in your bones you have to practice it all the time. You have to meditate or pray every day, and you have to stop many times during the day and remember to breathe. I have tried this. I am too distractible. Like Homer Simpson, I find myself humming "Turkey in the Straw" with stupid little cartoons playing in my head when I should be thinking about the beauty of the moment. I frequently end up thinking about sex. In short, I am just not spiritually advanced enough, or at least disciplined enough, to make myself sit quietly for half an hour a day. Which is a pretty sad statement, but there you go.

So I am walking home on this gorgeous day, and I am thinking that I know Kirsten is sick, I know things are tough, but I feel happy. And I start to congratulate myself. Maybe I have be-come a Zen master! Maybe, without any work at all, I have come to a point where I can appreciate a beautiful day just because it's a beautiful day, and I can be aware that Kirsten's life is in danger but still be completely happy to have her for today.

Well, needless to say, I soon pay for this spiritual hubris. I go home, and Kirsten is depressed. As we walk to Rowen's preschool to pick her up she tries to tell me what's wrong, and, like a clod, I say, just as she's starting to speak, "Ooh, look—looks like they sold one of these new condos!"

She glares at me and I fall all over myself apologizing for being such an oaf, and she tells me that she had a follow-up ap-pointment with Dr. J today, and it was not a good appointment.

"Why not?" I ask. "What happened?"

"Well, she did the examination, and she was like, 'I'd like to feel these lumps softening up a little more. Maybe we'll need to switch medicines for your next dose.'"

"Uh . . . meaning what?"

"Well, she said she wasn't sure, and they'd have to wait for the bloodwork—the woman who stuck me today was a total butcher, by the way, it totally killed—anyway, she thinks maybe this dose didn't work."

If you've been following me thus far, I'm sure you can guess that the bloodwork came back indicating that, in fact, this first medicine, the one that works for seventy percent of breast can-cers, seventy, mind you, seven-oh, did not work. This sucks. It sucks because Kirsten is bald and spent two weeks feeling really tired, and her cancer is still going strong.

It sucks because it is forcing me to face, once again, the possibility that she might die soon. I really have not allowed myself to think this at all, but this whole positive thinking thing turns out to be a house of cards based on Kirsten always being on the good side of these percentages because she is young and healthy. And yes, this is early in the treatment, but here she is in the bad thirty percent. What if we go through all this and she still dies? In our initial meeting with Dr. J, she told us that the lead patient out of her study is eight years on with no disease. Up until now I have been convinced that Kirsten will put this woman to shame, that she will undergo this treatment and beat her cancer like a rented mule until every single cell cries for mercy and then dies, and that we will be able to grow old together. But what if she doesn't? What then? How will I live? The last time I lived without her I was nineteen years old. I have no idea how to be an adult without this woman. I have no idea who I am without her.

Fuck.

Happy Birthday to Me

Kirsten is supposed to start her second round of chemo on my birthday, but it ends up being postponed from Monday to Thursday. My birthday is pretty uneventful, except that Kirsten makes me a yummy tray of brownies. During advisory period, which is kind of like homeroom, I let it slip that it's my birthday, and my advisees are all mad that I didn't tell them sooner. I tell them it's because, you know, I am the adult, and a lot of other advisors make a big deal of their advisees' birthdays, but I don't, and it would feel weird to me to have them make a big deal of my birthday. And it does feel a little weird, the next day, when they bring in chips and soda and a giant sheet cake decorated with "Happy Birthday Mr. Halpin," but I am really touched. It is one more example of people's tremendous kindness. It is especially nice because the ringleader is this girl who, I kid you not, got suspended fourteen times last year but managed to have the highest GPA in the school, and you may recall what Kirsten said to me about how I like smart troublemakers best. I spent at least an hour in meetings for each suspension in addition to numerous other meetings with her and/or her teachers, which was hard work, but I always felt like she was worth it, and this year she has become this model citizen. So this is probably the nicest thing that happens to me on my birthday.

And I think, well, a lot of my advisees have some tough stuff going on in their lives and they'd probably like for us all to make a big deal over their birthdays too, and I'm kind of a selfish shit for never arranging it. Oh well.

Kirsten has chemo on Thursday, and on Friday we head down to her parents' house for Birthday Fest 2000. Basically, Kirsten's uncle, aunt, brother, grandfather, and husband all have November birthdays, and so last summer Kirsten's dad got the idea to get everybody together for a big fiesta, and it was supposed to be in Florida where Kirsten's grandfather lives, but then Kirsten got diagnosed, so now it's in Massachusetts instead.

We get there and Kirsten almost immediately goes for a nap,

which lasts a couple of hours. I somehow find myself alone in the living room with Kirsten's uncle, who's a Republican, and her grandfather, who's . . . well, you know, "fascist" is a term that is really overused, but I do think it applies here, and he's also like eighty-five, so he can say whatever outrageous thing comes into his mind without fear of someone telling him to shut up.

Kirsten is snoozing, and the topic of the election comes up, and Kirsten's uncle says some predictably Republican things, which are annoying, but, okay, and her grandfather says something incoherent about Palm Beach and "Old Lieberstein, or whatever his name is . . . I guess Gore wanted the New York people . . ." and Kirsten's uncle, who is a Republican but not, as far as I can tell, a bigot, tries to steer this in a more acceptable direction by saying, "Yeah, I guess Gore wanted to appeal to the Northeast or something," but Gramps parries with, "Yeah! Northeast Israel!" and I get up and have to leave the room.

This birthday party is a very nice thing Kirsten's parents have done—I even got a customized souvenir hat for the occasion— but I am sort of on the outside looking in, because I'm not a blood relative and know Kirsten's aunts and uncles only about as well as you can know people you've met three times at various weddings, and also because all I want for my birthday is a healthy wife, and I can't have that, so I feel grumpy and not at all festive.

And I have to doff my souvenir cap to the whole family, because Kirsten was sort of dreading this, and even told me that my role during this whole event was to keep her from snapping at people, but the family handle it perfectly. They acknowledge that she's bald, and Gramps even teases her about it, but they don't fawn, and nobody clutches either of us by the arm, looks meaningfully at us, and says, "So how *are* you," or anything like that. We're just at a party, and yes it's a party that's been moved a thousand miles just so we can be there, but we are not the stars, and that is wonderful.

Which is not to say that I have any fun. After a few hours, the Slide Show starts. Now, I have sat through the Slide Show a few times in the past, and the first time it was entertaining, because I hadn't seen all these pictures of Kirsten as a kid, and it is always fun to see how awful people looked in the 1970s, and it's funny when Kirsten's dad embarrasses her mom with that picture of her bending over, and the second time it was mildly amusing, and this time . . . well, I am cranky already, and there are twelve carousels of slides to get through. Twelve.

After the first four, I head off to take a nap, and I am almost asleep when Rowen comes out to the couch, climbs up, and begins to jump up and down on my rib cage. I bark something at her and she runs back to the Slide Show crying, she is crushed, and though my reaction is not really inappropriate to having somebody unexpectedly stomp on you when you are half asleep, I made my daughter cry, and I feel like a total asshole. We eventually make up and end up playing while the Slide Show goes on, and we take a cake break and then head home before they've even gotten to carousel eleven.

You Must Be Angry

I talk to my mom a lot. I always have. I love my mom, and I even like her, which seems like a relatively rare gift, but she still gets on my nerves sometimes in that mom way. I am, however, perfectly willing to admit that this is at least half my fault. You know how it is—your friend could say something to you, and you'd react like, "Wow, that's great advice—my friend is so wise," but if your mom said the exact same words, you'd react like, "Jeez, mom! Shut up! Let me live my own life!"

So when my mom ventures into the spiritual realm, I get kind of annoyed. In our initial conversations after the diagnosis, she said that she hopes I'm not mad at God. Now, to be honest, except for the Keith Richards thing, I am really not mad at God, but I kind of feel like I should defend that position once my mom stakes out the opposite one. So we have a short talk about this, and she can tell I'm getting annoyed, so she backs off, but not before telling me that she hopes I don't think I'm cursed or something, but that shit just happens. Now, I do find it pretty hard to square the idea of a just and loving God with a lot of the horrible suffering that goes on in the world, much of it worse than mine, but I decide to let it lie.

It doesn't come up again until weeks later, when she asks how I'm feeling, and I say sad, and she says, "Well, you must be feeling a lot of anger," and I say I'm really not, and she says, "Well, I mean the unfairness of it all must be making you angry," and I say, "No, I'm really not angry, I'm just sad," and I think but don't say, "Jeez! Three weeks ago you didn't want me to be angry, and now you want me to be angry! What the hell!"

I have told her the truth. I am really not angry at all. I think maybe I get to skip this stage. When your dad falls over dead for no reason when you are nine years old, that strips you of your feeling of invulnerability pretty quickly. I remember thinking when my dad died that this kind of thing didn't happen to me, but I got over that pretty quickly. So I think most people feel invulnerable to tragedy until their first tragedy strikes, and then they get angry. I've already had my first tragedy, so this time around I had no illusions that I was in some way protected from this kind of thing. In fact, I am so keenly aware that tragedy doesn't have any special reason to avoid me that I spent a lot of time when I was happy waiting for the other shoe to drop. When Rowen was born healthy, and I finally landed a job at a small school in the city, and we made a bucketload of money selling a condo above a lunatic, I felt uneasy. It seemed like it was all too good to be true. And, as it turns out, I was right.

So I am not outraged, I am not shocked, I am not surprised. I'm just kind of sad and resigned. Here we go again.

Okay, Maybe I Am Angry

The worst part about being a teacher is not the kids. The kids are the best part, the whole reason why I love to get up and go to work early in the morning. Anybody who feels that the kids are the worst part of being a teacher should stop being a teacher.

No, the worst part of being a teacher is the grown-ups. In many other places I worked, it was many of my colleagues, but I am lucky now to work in a place where my colleagues are not a huge pain in the ass, and even the ones I disagree with a lot I respect for their commitment to their work.

But today for our faculty meeting we have a presentation by some education consultant, and these things are always horrible. I try very hard to keep an open mind, but I have been to enough of these things to know that they always suck: either you have someone reading incredibly boring shit off of overheads, or you break into small groups and talk about something pointless and write the results on big pieces of paper that you then post on the wall and discuss.

I also have to say that I have a prejudice against education consultants. They are all former teachers who couldn't hack it for one reason or another and decided that their failure to make a career of teaching, along with the MBA or other degree they subsequently earned, gave them the expertise to go around the country charging huge fees to tell teachers what to do. I guess it's nice work if you can get it, but to me it ranks below pornographer on the list of honest occupations that contribute something valuable to society. Which of course means that like pornographers, education consultants make much more money than teachers.

So I walk into this presentation feeling a little grumpy, but I try to keep an open mind, because you can usually get at least one valuable thing out of even the most stultifying presentation, but this one sucks from the start. What the guy basically suggests, after saying that our youth need to be developed, and that this means they have to do calculus in the twelfth grade (I have never taken calculus and am therefore, I guess, undeveloped and not truly free. Or something), with his jargon-laden PowerPoint slides, is that the existence of excellent teachers proves that everyone who's not an excellent teacher could be if they just used his process.

After saying that his presentation is interactive, the consultant gets really defensive when we challenge anything he says, and he cuts us off and is generally disrespectful, and after one of my colleagues suggests that sometimes kids who can learn come into the classroom with a lot of baggage for whatever reason and that we need to figure out how to help them with that stuff too, he gets all huffy and says he is not going to spend his time talking about how this can't be done, and that he doesn't believe everyone in this room really believes in the kids, and that the people who complain the most are often the people who are struggling the most, while the people who still have that spark are sitting silent. I happen to know that the people who are sitting silent are actually passing notes about how insulting this presentation is, but I have been one of the people speaking up the most, so his point to me is clear. I get up and walk out of the presentation and find myself fairly shaking with rage.

I go sit in the nurse's office and vent about some guy who doesn't teach coming in here and questioning my commitment to my career because I didn't swallow all of his bullshit. Would I always have been this angry about something like this? Probably, but in the past I would have most likely kept sitting there. Am I courageous, or just a crank? Within about two minutes of venting, the nurse asks me how Kirsten is doing, and I find myself crying. So it's all related somehow. Am I quicker to anger because of this? Am I quicker to walk out on something stupid because the seriousness of what's happening to Kirsten has given me a "what the fuck" attitude about other stuff? I don't know. All I know is that I am sad and that maybe I was lying when I told my mom I wasn't angry.

Rough Justice

I have been working on this theory that your punishment for making fun of someone is that, sooner or later, you become them. I know this doesn't square with what I've said earlier about God only intervening in the world through people, but it seems like a pretty ironclad law of the universe.

Here is a partial list of people I have made fun of and subsequently become:

Dorky alumni who walk around your college campus buying crisp new sweatshirts for their toddlers.

People who like country music.

People who like punk rock.

People who revere Prince.

Adults who own video game systems. (This one is particularly egregious—Kirsten's brother camped out at Wal-Mart to buy a PlayStation 2, so we naturally made fun of him, and less than a week later I was asking if he would give me his old PlayStation.)

People who talk on cell phones walking down the street or standing on the subway platform. Yep. I've done both.

Parents who talk incessantly about their cute kids.

Vegetarians.

Churchgoers.

The list could go on, but I guess you get the idea. Basically the only group of people I have made fun of on a consistent basis and have yet to become are Deadheads/Phish heads. So by the time you read this I will probably be in Vermont, dorky Ecuadoran hat on head, unkempt beard down to mid-chest, stoned out of my mind and thinking it's cool that I paid thirty bucks to watch some guy play a vacuum cleaner.

The thing is, I don't remember ever making fun of cancer patients or their spouses. Go figure.

PlayStation

As I previously mentioned, I was able to overcome Kirsten's resistance to having video games in the house with a lot of pathetic pleading and with the serendipitous fact of her brother, Andrew, suddenly having an obsolete PlayStation on his hands.

What I basically said was that, you know, this was a very stressful time for me, and when she is feeling crappy and goes to bed at eight o'clock, I have two hours to kill, during which time I could, theoretically, read, but I don't seem to have the patience right now, or I can watch TV, and TV right now totally sucks . . .

Well, okay, it has probably always totally sucked, but my tolerance for it right now is very low. Of course I still love *The Simpsons,* I like watching football on Sunday, and I would watch the Celtics if I thought they were not on the road to suckitude again, but that appears unlikely.

One of the reasons I lobby so hard for the video games is that I grew up with them, and they feel like comfort food for my brain. I was one of those kids who used to spend rolls of quarters on Space Invaders, Galaxian, and lesser-known classics like Red Baron, which is about the only game I was ever really good at. Even in college I used to sneak away to the arcade from time to time for a game of Teenage Mutant Ninja Turtles, or play the ancient Dig Dug game that was in the basement of our dorm. So right now when things are really shitty, maybe I am regressing. Or maybe I have only been pretending to be over video games for the last ten years. It's probably both.

So Kirsten caves, and we have her brother, Andrew, and sister-in-law, Keri, over for dinner, and they give me the PlayStation and we hook it up after Rowen goes to bed. (Two things I have promised: no playing while Rowen is awake, which I am sure will be violated before this whole thing is over, and no shooting games, which I am pretty sure will not be violated, even though shooting games are really fun. I am enough of an old man and have taken enough of Thich Nhat Hanh to heart to be somewhat disturbed about casting myself in the role of someone essentially on a killing spree.) They give me a racing game, because I said I couldn't really handle anything brainy right now where I have to, you know, find the seven keys to unlock the wizard's sock drawer or whatever.

The game is hard and really fun, and every night for the next three nights I sit there patiently racing that Audi TT, which is a car I do sort of lust for in real life, and never getting a better result than second, but it is a blast, even if it is kind of antisocial, and I have now actually started reading a book that I like and I feel kind of guilty about spending all my time racing, and I have also been working on writing this and feeling guilty about racing instead.

But the thing is, it doesn't seem to work much as a stress-buster. I play until bedtime and am totally wired. I fall asleep but wake up a lot with visions of races playing in my head, and I sleep fitfully and feel like shit the next day. And I can't wait to play again. I am guessing this must be sort of how crack addicts feel.

Anyway, surprise surprise, while I will certainly get a lot of enjoyment out of this machine (thank you, Andrew), it isn't the solution. It isn't going to get me through this. Owning stuff, even really cool stuff, isn't going to get me through this. I wonder what will.

The Day Before Thanksgiving

Wednesday before Thanksgiving I have a half-day at work, and these days are almost always terrible, but today it's not. My students are working on performing scenes from *Romeo and Juliet,* and we spend our eighty-minute class period rehearsing and giving people feedback on their scenes right up until dismissal time, and I believe this is the first time in my eight years of teaching that I have felt like I had a really good and productive day on the Wednesday before Thanksgiving.

I head home early to meet Kirsten and we head down to Blockbuster so I can rent PlayStation games. I quickly discover the ultimate joy and horror of this experience. The joy is that they have a ton of games, and you can play them for four bucks instead of forty, and if you come across one that really sucks, you don't feel like you got royally screwed. The pain is that they give you the game without any instruction booklet. Now, I'm sure that your average twelve-year-old finds this no impediment at all to his enjoyment, but to a man of my age it is daunting to face this controller with twelve buttons and two joysticks without any indication of how I'm supposed to use them. I end up getting a snowboarding game that proves to be completely baffling.

We go to a great secondhand clothing store where we get a lot of Rowen's clothes because she needs a jacket. We find one for six bucks, and I also find a heavyweight Champion sweatshirt bearing the name of a school I actually attended, also for six bucks. We continue on, stopping at the auto parts store to get a replacement headlight (I have been driving around with a pa-diddle for about three weeks now, and this is much more humiliating than the fact that the door to my gas tank won't close and flaps in the wind or the fact that the car is covered in birdshit from parking under a tree) and a replacement bulb for our inside light, which has been burned out for at least two years. What can I say, it just never seemed urgent.

We then head over to the only one of the three all-vegetarian restaurants in town that we have never tried. The other two are run by the same people and are good but overly greasy Chinese-Vietnamese food with dingy atmosphere and indifferent service. This place, on the other hand, is beautiful on the inside, the service is friendly and relatively good, and the food is celestial. We spend the whole meal going, "Wow, this place is beautiful . . . so much nicer than the other place . . . The bathroom here isn't a filthy hellhole like the other place . . . Ooh, try this, it's delicious . . ."

It is really nice to have a date with Kirsten. Even running errands with just the two of us is a wonderful change, something we get to do very rarely. It is a lot of fun. We laugh, we make jokes, we gush over how great the food is. She is my best friend, and I love just hanging around with her. It is something we don't get to do often enough, even before she got sick. Much of the time it feels like we are co-workers in the child-rearing workplace, and, you know, it's a fun job, but it's also nice to remember why we got married in the first place.

We come home and, like a fool, I start looking through these children's books that Kirsten's friend Jen got for us. Mind you, we asked her to look for this kind of thing, so she came through. They are books about kids whose parents have cancer, and I knew they existed, but they are tough to find. There are like a million books about kids getting sick and being hospitalized, mostly from the 1970s and mostly having to do with getting tonsils taken out, which is something that I am sure the HMOs make them do in the office with a hot pair of tweezers these days anyway, but the books about sick parents are hard to find. We thought that seeing her experience reflected in a book might help Rowen feel that what she was going through was normal, just like having your home invaded by a puckish, bipedal talking cat or other such normal stuff you find in children's books.

So I read through one, and it's about this girl and how her mom loses her hair, and how she remembers cheering her mom on in some 10K race and now she can't get out of bed, and in the end she starts to get better, but she says she can't promise that she won't be sick anymore. And I start to sob. Now, I'm not talking about the stoic, tear-rolling-down-the-cheek kind of crying I did, for example, while watching *Romeo and Juliet* with my class, nor am I talking about the more expressive twisted-mouth crying I often allow myself while I am walking to work and no one's around. No, I am talking about full-on, out-of-control sobbing. You know the "Ahheeeeeeeehh . . . heeeeeennnnhhhh . . . heeeeeeeenh" my-heart's-being-ripped-out kind of sobbing that, if you're lucky, you have not done very much as an adult. And which I have not allowed myself to do since this whole thing started.

Kirsten comforts me, and I apologize, because, you know, she's doing my job and I'm doing hers right now, and she says it's okay, but I can't stop sobbing, and the thing is that the vocalization that accompanies it is strangely high-pitched. What I'm trying to say is that I sound like a girl. A little girl. And it just kind of strikes me as funny, and I manage to sob out, "Don't know why . . . can't stop crying like a girl . . . ," and this strikes me as really funny, and then I start to laugh hysterically, and this is also not the manliest sound, totally "hee-hee-hee-hee-hee" kind of laughing rather than hearty "ha ha ha"s, and it strikes me that my laughter sounds just like my crying, and I keep alternating between hysterical sobs and hysterical laughter, and I guess that just about sums up what it's like to be me these days.

Neil Peart's Blues

I keep being reminded that making fun of someone makes you become them. No, I haven't bought Phish tickets or any Ecuadoran knitted goods yet, but I know that the group of people I have probably been harshest on during this whole thing are people who are going through something similar but not as severe. I have written several snide and shitty things about them, and at one point my mom sent me something that some guy had written for one of the Sunday insert magazines about how he dealt with his wife's lumpectomy. Lumpectomy, yet! It talked about how he comforted his wife and assured her that she wouldn't lose her hair from the chemo, and my reaction at the time was, "Shut the fuck up, you fuckin' pussy!" (To get the full effect you have to do it in the Southwestern Ohio rural accent, because that is the accent in which those words were frequently hurled at me as a youth.) "What I wouldn't give to have Kirsten have a fucking lumpectomy! Don't talk to me about losing hair, man, we're worried about her losing her fucking life!"

Okay. So then yesterday I am reading in the paper about Geddy Lee's new solo album. Let me say as an aside that I was listening to Rush when we had our marathon appointment with Dr. J. Well, not during the appointment, except when they drew the curtain and felt Kirsten up and I needed to feel like I was somewhere else. I found listening to "Red Barchetta" very comforting because a) it fuckin' rocks, dude! and b) it sort of reminds me of middle school. Now you know I'm in the midst of a horrible experience if reminding myself of the hormonal hell that was middle school is comforting by comparison.

Anyway, so why is Geddy Lee putting out a solo album? Well, it turns out that Rush is kind of on hold because drummer Neil Peart lost his only child in a car wreck and his wife to cancer in the space of like a year. And so that kind of puts me in my place. I mean this in the nicest way, Neil, and I am glad you're still with us, but I really think I would've killed myself. Well, actually I know I am way too cowardly to kill myself, but I look at where I am and where Neil Peart is and all I can think of is him reading this and going, "Shut the fuck up, you fuckin' pussy!"

Some Good News at Last

After telling her that her first round of chemo didn't work, Dr. J schedules her for a second round that involves some kind of speedball of two drugs that have a synergistic effect, or something. I get all this secondhand because I don't go to any of Kirsten's appointments. Her mom and her friend Olga go with her a lot, and I go to work. It is okay because her mom really wants to go and, as I've said, I hate to leave work, and Kirsten doesn't seem to mind, so everybody's happy. Well, actually, everybody's kind of miserable, but you know what I mean.

Dr. J also tells Kirsten that they want to get two rounds of chemo that work under her belt before she is hospitalized, so her hospitalization will be pushed back by three weeks. This is a big blow to us, because we were starting to make plans and my mom was on the verge of buying a plane ticket, but more importantly, we were just getting psyched to be done with this. Now there is more waiting, which is what so much of this has been. Waiting for test results, waiting to see if the chemo worked, waiting in waiting rooms, waiting in examining rooms, waiting for phone calls.

Kirsten has her second round of chemo, and once again she tolerates it really well and doesn't puke at all. She's kind of tired all the time but not dishrag-on-the-couch tired. I have lots of blank days and a few angry days. Eventually it is time for her follow-up appointment, and this is when we will finally find out if this second round worked or not.

I have been tying myself in knots wondering what would happen if the second round didn't work. I am sure it would involve switching up medicines and postponing the hospitalization again, but it would be another setback, and it would suck. Bad news is starting to feel inevitable, because every time there has been a possibility of good news or bad news, we have gotten bad news. I am getting pretty fucking sick of the tiger, and I really want the lady, but the fact that the tiger keeps coming up makes it seem like it will again.

Kirsten goes for her appointment, and it turns out that Dr. J is overbooked or something. I didn't realize that doctors worked like airlines, but apparently they do, except, you know, you never have the hope of getting bumped to first class, or getting a free drink, and you damn sure don't want a free ticket for next time. They take blood and another doctor examines her, and this is not really helpful because this doctor has never examined her before, so she doesn't have any baseline, and Kirsten says that she thinks her tumors are shrinking, and the doctor makes some noncommittal noises, so we have to wait for the bloodwork, which takes a couple of days.

At the end of our nice day before Thanksgiving, Marie the oncology nurse calls and says the first tumor marker has come back down a little and Dr. J wants to see Kirsten next week. We don't really know what to make of this news. It is certainly good news that it's down, but Dr. J said she wanted to see the number cut in half, and Marie just said it's down slightly. Still, the fact that it's down at all seems good, and coupled with the fact that Kirsten thinks her tumors are shrinking, this must mean it's working. Right?

The night before Kirsten's appointment with Dr. J, I sleep like absolute shit. I fall into bed exhausted at 10:00 because I was at work late watching my students perform scenes from *Romeo and Juliet.* And I bolt awake at 12:30, with snatches of lines from the play going through my mind ("too flattering sweet to be substantial" gets big airplay for some reason) along with snatches of songs and other stupid sounds and thoughts. I am not worrying, I don't feel nervous. I just can't sleep. I get up and turn on the TV and watch some ads for some really remarkable and amazing new products, and catch a couple of minutes of *Car Wash,* which is like this amazing 1970s time capsule with giant-Afroed men, stereotyped black revolutionaries, stereotyped rich kid revolutionaries, and *Starsky and Hutch's* Huggy Bear, Antonio Fargas, as the stereotyped, scarf-bedecked gay man, who, in the few minutes I watched, told the angry stereotyped revolutionary: "I'm more man than you'll ever be and more woman than you'll ever get!" Meow!

I finally fall back asleep at 3:30, and I am up again at 5:30. Kirsten's dad has stayed over and comes out of the bathroom naked and asks me for a towel and I am humbled by the fact that he is sixty-two and looks way better naked than I do. I go to work and still feel like complete shit, and many cups of tea and some positively sludgy Puerto Rican coffee that one of my colleagues brews up for our department meeting don't help.

While I'm practically dead by the time I get home, Kirsten is bouncing off the walls. "How was your appointment?" I ask. Today is the day of another big follow-up appointment with Dr. J. I didn't go because we are anticipating that I'm going to need to miss a lot of work, so we are trying to save up my absences for when she is totally incapacitated. This is Kirsten's idea, but I am all too happy to go along with it.

"It was really really good," she says. "First of all, the woman who drew my blood was an *artist*. I felt *nothing*. And then Dr. J did the examination, and she said the tumors were definitely shrinking, and one tumor marker is up, but she thinks that's just because, I dunno, one of the tumors is breaking up, and there might be big pieces floating around in my blood or something gross like that. So then she said, 'Well, since this is working, let's not wait, let's get you into the hospital next week.' "

Kirsten is practically walking on air, and I am too. All my fatigue and worry just completely fall away. I had been ready to fall over, and now I am bouncing off the walls. It's amazing what comes to pass for good news, but I am ecstatic that they are going to take my wife away for three weeks next week and give her so much deadly medicine that they will completely destroy her immune system and ability to make blood and that I'm going to have to live with some combination of my mother-in-law and my mother during this time. This is fucking fantastic news. At last we're really doing it. I feel like Sherlock Holmes, shouting, "The game's afoot!"

Crushin'

My hormones are out of control. I mean, yes, always, as a rule, but right now especially. This is, I am sure, partly due to the fact that, you know, chemo and sex don't exactly mix, but I think there is that old fear-of-death/desire-for-sex thing, and I have been terribly afraid of losing Kirsten while waiting to find out if the second round of chemo worked, and I am just looking at other women all the time, even more than usual.

Now, I've always been this way to a degree, and I justify it by imagining that everybody else is like this (and an unscientific poll of everyone I know who is married shows this to be true), that being married doesn't stop you from being attracted to other people, it just (hopefully) stops you from acting on that attraction.

So I periodically get meaningless crushes, and I know that they are meaningless crushes, and we are secure enough in our relationship at this point that we can joke about our crushes, as long as they are on celebrities, so when I beg to go see *Charlie's Angels,* Kirsten finally says, "Okay. As long as you promise not to drool openly over Drew Barrymore." (I manage, but just barely. She's dreamy! And the movie kicks ass!) And I can tease Kirsten about her frequent trips to the pizza place for an eggplant parm sub and her crush on the guy who works there with the enormous tattooed biceps. Yeah, I know he's not a celebrity, but he's not somebody we really know, and he's probably about as accessible to Kirsten as Drew Barrymore is to me. (She's so dreamy!)

We are not yet to the point where we can joke about our crushes on people we actually know, though. When it became obvious several years ago that Kirsten had a crush on some British, motorcycle-riding co-worker with numerous piercings, I got cranky about it, and I never mention my work crushes. Right now I have moderate crushes on three women at work, two of whom are attached and one of whom I think is probably a lesbian. I also have crushes on two moms and one teacher at Rowen's preschool. All are married or attached. Some woman who used to work at my school and who I should in fairness, after mocking Kirsten's crush, admit has multiple piercings stops by my classroom to borrow books and we have some kind of interaction that she probably doesn't think anything of but I think is flirtatious because she smiles at me a lot, and my students tease me and say they're going to tell my wife, and I say, "You don't have to tell her I'm the mack! She knows that already!"

But that night when the students are doing their *Romeo and Juliet* scenes, Kirsten shows up with Rowen, and Rowen is wearing a fancy dress that Kirsten's parents bought her and Kirsten is wearing her wig, which is called "The Cory" but which we call "The Velma" because it looks kind of like Velma's hair from *Scooby-Doo*. I know this sounds corny and probably unbelievable in light of everything I've just said, but it is absolutely true that the whole rest of the room just falls away because my whole life just walked in the door, and I hug and kiss them both.

The next day we are doing a lesson on adverbs and I ask the kids to add an adverb to the sentence "Diana kissed Dwayne _____" and somebody says, "hotly," and one of the students says, "Ooo, I saw Mr. Halpin kiss his wife hotly last night," and I say, because propriety was never my strong suit, and I am sleep-deprived, "Girl, that wasn't *even* hotly," and this gets a chorus of "Oooooooo"s and "He means they kiss hotter than that!"s. The bottom line is that I love her so much and just want her back. I want her to be cured and live and live and live.

Me and Rowen Down by the Schoolyard

Rowen and I have been spending a lot of time together over the last few weeks. We both get up early, while Kirsten likes to sleep late even when she's not having her body ravaged by chemo, so we hang out and play, or we go grocery shopping, or we go to the playground. One day we go over to the park across the street and I take the video camera that Joe and Katy lent us so I can practice with it, because the plan is to videotape Rowen while Kirsten is in the hospital. My showing up with a video camera has the happy side effect of driving away the guys getting high on the bench behind the swings, but mostly we just have a great time playing.

Though I never again get to play the accidental crimebuster, Rowen and I have many other fun activities together while Kirsten is feeling kind of shitty. I find it impossible to explain why I have so much fun with her without starting to sound like a precious moments greeting card or something: "DAUGH-TER: The time we spend together is so special. I love your laughter and your little smile. I love the fact that you're my little angel. And I love that you are growing all the while . . ." Okay, not really that pukey, but close enough to make me uncomfortable. So let me just say that she is incredibly funny and I really enjoy her company. One day we go to the Children's Museum, and in the little kids' area they have these tables piled high with shaving cream and food coloring, and we spend probably an hour there just making little shaving cream mountains, writing in the shaving cream, and laughing our asses off as we gradually get covered with green and yellow foam. It is one of those moments of perfect happiness that I already get misty-eyed when I look back at, and that I will probably talk about when she is sixteen while she rolls her eyes and yanks the car keys out of my hands.

The two of us have a great time together. But all the while, while I am doing things like showing her the revolting jar of lamb's tongues at the supermarket and saying, "Should we get this?" and she knows her part perfectly and acts like she thinks I'm serious and says, "No way!" or while we are picking out treats for Kirsten or while we are enjoying a hot beverage and a baked good, I feel like there are two clouds hanging over us. The first one is the cloud of Kirsten's impending hospitalization. What is it going to be like when I am the only parent around? Will we still have fun, or will it be horrible, like when I pick her up from school without Kirsten and she spends the entire walk home going, "Mommmmm-yyyyyyyyyy . . . mommmmmmmmm-yyyyyyyyy"?

Cloud two, of course, is the cloud of us having to do this for the rest of our lives with no Kirsten. What would that be like? Sometimes I feel that we could get through it, you know, me and you, kid, against the world, but then I remember what it was like being the kid in that scenario, and while I certainly feel like my mom and I got through, I also think it kind of fucked up our relationship. I mean—just the two of us together for nine years after my dad died—it was very intense. By the time I was in college, we were driving each other insane. I am sure that's true of many kids and parents who haven't endured a tragedy together, so maybe there's no cause and effect here, but why do I live eight hundred miles from my mom? Why don't I feel any need to live closer to her? What if that happens with Rowen and me? It would break my heart. I know it hurts my mom.

The line I use in conversation these days talking about this fear is, "I was always so afraid of ending up like my dad that I never bothered to worry about ending up like my mom." It doesn't get laughs, except from me, and I'm just laughing nervously to cover my fear.

Powerpuff

While we are waiting for Kirsten to go into the hospital, I suddenly become obsessed with the Powerpuff Girls. Rowen is a huge fan, as is every girl at her school. Basically *The Powerpuff Girls* is a cartoon about three kindergarten-aged superhero girls who kick lots of ass, especially the ass of their unaccountably Japanese-accented nemesis, the evil chimp genius Mojo Jojo. The other girls at Rowen's school were all very into this and had lots of merchandise, and, fearing that our little angel would become a social leper if she didn't learn the names of the characters and a few scenarios to act out when they play this on the playground, which is at least twice a day, we went out and bought a couple of videos. The other option was shelling out for more-than-basic cable, and I know this makes me some kind of Luddite crank, but I just feel like a jackass paying somebody fifty bucks a month to deliver TV with commercials.

So Rowen likes to watch the videos, and one day we subject our friends Joe and Katy to a viewing that includes my favorite episode, in which Rainbow the Clown is doused in bleach, becomes Mr. Mime, and turns the city black and white until the Powerpuff Girls restore color to the world by playing a really catchy pop tune called "Love Makes the World Go Round." Blossom transforms Mr. Mime back into Rainbow the Clown with a guitar solo played on what looks like a Gibson Flying V, which is a guitar so stupid-looking that only cartoon characters and heavy metal guitarists (I know, I know, same thing) should play it. After they finish the song, which, I remind you, is called "Love Makes the World Go Round," Rainbow the Clown thanks them for restoring him to his true self, and they beat the shit out of him.

Anyway, some time after this, Joe sends me a CD of songs "Inspired by the Powerpuff Girls." (By this time I have put the Carter Family aside for a while and have been alternating between Matthew Sweet's melancholy pop masterpiece *100% Fun* and the first Stooges album, which has the song "No Fun," which I play over and over for reasons that are probably obvious.) I am immediately put off by the new CD, probably because I have been burned on compilation CDs a number of times. In fact I have been burned so often by tribute CDs that I now avoid them like the plague. A bunch of bands with stupid names who think they're clever deliver inferior versions of songs by an artist you like. Who needs it? But this is not a tribute to a recording artist, so I pop it in and find that I love it. Yes, it does have bands with stupid names (Bis?? What the hell is Bis?), but for some reason I can't stop listening to it.

I mean, I become obsessed with this CD more than I have with anything else in years with the exception of the Carter Family. For about a week and a half it is all I can stand to listen to. I listen on the walk to work, and as Shonen Knife belt out their ode to Buttercup, the Powerpuff Girl with the bad attitude, tears come to my eyes. I mean literally. I am listening to the female Japanese equivalent of the Ramones sing about a cartoon character, and I start to cry. What the fuck is wrong with me?

Well, besides the fact that my life has completely turned inside out and my best friend in the world is about to go into the hospital to receive a deadly dose of life-giving medicine? I don't know. For some reason my emotional pendulum has swung completely away from the Carter Family, and I no longer want to hear anything about jilted lovers killing themselves; I just want to hear about cartoon little girls kicking a monkey's ass. Is it because I associate Rowen with the Powerpuff Girls, and the Shonen Knife song is just this unremittingly positive tune about a little girl who can't be stopped? I think that's partly it. I think it's also just that the whole thing is so appealing: living in a world where your greatest worry is that you'll have to fight the same psychotic monkey whose ass you kicked last week again and will kick again this week. It's so unlike my life right now. And because it is a beautiful vision, or because it is so far removed from reality, I love it.

Making Plans for Kirsten

Elation quickly turns to dread as Kirsten's hospitalization approaches. I mean, we are still glad that she is going in and getting started on her treatment, but I am starting to think about how incredibly much it's going to suck to have her in the hospital for three weeks, and how it's going to make me sad, and I wonder if Rowen is going to freak out.

Kirsten's mom is freaking out already. Not, you know, in a real emotional freakout way, but in a planning way. I swear she calls us at least three times a day, going, "What's the plan, what's the plan?" Once she calls at 9:00 P.M., which is damn close to bedtime around here, and then at 8:00 the next morning.

And it's all Kirsten can do to be civil and explain that no, we still don't know exactly when Brendan's mom is coming, we still don't know all the details of the hospitalization, relax and we'll call you soon. Again, the impulse is good—she wants to be helpful and she wants to know what's happening, and yet for some reason it's annoying.

I get increasingly grumpy, and I am especially worried about what's going to happen with Rowen. The day before my school's parents' night, which I am going to blow off because I'll be taking Kirsten to the hospital, the five of us who share a classroom get an e-mail from the principal telling us very nicely that the room is a sty and we need to clean it up before parents come in. I think he is very nice to address the e-mail to everyone, because I know that it's really my fault. I have stacks of shit on top of my desk in ugly, chaotic piles, many of which are precariously balanced on top of two books, or a coffee mug, or some souvenir one of my advisees gave me. Next to my desk is a pile of books I never quite got around to shelving. And the bookshelf where my students' independent reading books are housed is a complete mess, with books stacked on top of each other, sticking out at odd angles. These are the three worst aesthetic crimes in the room, and they are all mine. And I really wish I could claim that, you know, my wife is sick and I'm not paying the kind of attention to these things that I usually do, but the fact is that I'm just a fucking slob, and it was like this last year too.

So I take it upon myself to do most of the cleaning, and at one point I find an umbrella. "Anybody want an umbrella?" I ask, and one of my co-workers says, "Yeah. Does it work?" so I open it. It does work. One of my favorite students, who is of

Haitian descent, is sitting there while this whole umbrella thing happens, and she says, "Opening an umbrella inside. Bad luck. Bad luck." I look at her and say, "Josette, my wife has cancer. How much worse could my luck get?"

She pauses for a moment and answers, with a totally straight face, "You could turn black . . ."

And I know that I am her teacher and should spend at least an hour deconstructing the history of internalized racism behind that joke, but all I can do is laugh my ass off. It just paralyzes me.

No Glove, No Love

Wednesday is the big day that Kirsten goes into the bubble. I get a nice card from my advisees telling me that it's all going to be okay and that they are praying for me and my wife, and I am incredibly touched. I remark on the fact that it's kind of back-asswards that the sixteen-year-olds are supporting me, when that is what I am supposed to do for them, but they look at me like I'm an idiot. I guess I am. I have tried like hell for over a year to bring this group together, and in some weird way, I think I have finally done it. I'm grateful to be able to see them every day, and my gratitude for their ongoing kindness to me has not, thus far, stopped me from busting their asses about their grades, so that's good.

I leave work in the middle of the day and walk over to the hospital to meet Kirsten. As I walk, I think about how I have all these positive associations with this hospital. Since Rowen was born here, I sort of think of it as a place where wonderful things happen. I hope something wonderful happens this time. We meet in the lobby and head up to the bubble. It's not really a plastic bubble like in the old John Travolta TV movie, but you do have to go through this airlock to get to the hallway where her room is, and we immediately associated it with that movie as soon as it was described to us, so we have been talking for weeks about "when you go into the bubble." We go through one set of automatic doors and have to stand there and wait for the doors behind us to close before the next set opens.

Inside the bubble floor we meet Kirsten's nurse, who is very nice and takes us to the sad little lounge. I spy a *People* magazine of recent vintage, but I'm pretty sure it doesn't count, since this is a patient lounge rather than a waiting room. Odds are a patient left it here. There are also two TVs, and as we sit there waiting, a sad-looking older man sits there trying to get the news to come in on one of them, but neither one seems equipped to pick up any channels. This is a horrible thing that happened to TVs some time when I wasn't looking. All of a sudden you need extra equipment to make a TV pick up TV stations. Strange.

Anyway, I hear the guy say that they are working on his wife so he can't be in the room, and his wife is here for a bone marrow transplant, and I know I should feel like he is my brother, but I just don't. I don't hate or resent him for being older and going through this, and presumably having had many cancer-free years with his wife. I guess I just look at this guy in his sixties and figure, well, he's the guy who's *supposed* to be here. What the hell am *I* doing here? I feel for him, because he's obviously sad, but so am I, and I just don't want to talk to anybody else who's sad right now. I don't want to talk to anyone who knows what I'm going through.

The nurse takes three vials of blood from Kirsten because, she explains, Phlebotomy is delayed and they won't be here for an hour. I have no fucking idea who Phlebotomy is or why it would take them so long to get here. I mean, it's a big hospital and everything, but it's not *that* big.

Kirsten is supposed to get "bedside surgery" today to implant a new hose in her chest—this one is a four-in-one!—and they tell her that the surgeon who was scheduled to do this went home sick. Great. So they are looking for another surgeon. After they leave, I say, "Well, we're in a hospital, I guess there must be one or two around," and Kirsten says she thinks it's not that simple.

They send us off to lunch so they can hunt down a surgeon, so we head off to the local brewpub in search of fries. I don't mean to harp on the whole Irish heritage thing too much, but fried potatoes and beer just make my blood sing with joy, and I guess that's as good an explanation as any.

I order the imperial stout, and, since I am somewhat of a beer geek, I know that imperial stout is a special kind of extra-high-alcohol stout, presumably because that's what the emperor wants, needs, or deserves, or something. I guess the serfs drank Bud Light or something.

Anyway, the imperial stout totally kicks my ass, and even though we order an extra plate of fries after we finish the ones that came with my sandwich, I can't eat enough food to compete with the kick this beer delivers. The buzz will last all afternoon, and I will be damn glad it does. I have no way of knowing this when I place the order, but I am really going to need that extra-drunk feeling that a strong beer in the daytime provides.

We head back to the hospital, and I return to the patient lounge while Kirsten gets ready. This involves her scrubbing herself from head to toe with antibacterial soap and getting into the hospital clothes. While I sit there, another patient, a Chinese man in his twenties, comes in and pops a movie into the VCR. It is some kind of Hong Kong comedy-adventure, and I can read just enough of the subtitles from where I'm sitting to see that it's about an idiot-savant type of guy who becomes this accidental crime lord. In one scene, he asks a rival crime lord to tie his shoes, and everyone is shocked at this blatant sign of contempt and disrespect that's sure to cause a gang war, but the guy really didn't know how to tie his shoes. So it's that kind of movie. I can totally understand why this guy, who is also having a bone marrow transplant or he wouldn't be here in a fabulous light blue johnny, wants to spend his days watching this. So do I.

But Kirsten is out of the shower, so I will never know how the movie ends, though I suspect that the fact that the idiot-savant guy can shoot a gun with deadly accuracy becomes important later on in the movie.

We both enter the bubble room, and for the first time I go through the ritual I will go through at least once a day for the next three weeks. I remove my coat and bag and leave them in a drawer outside the room. Immediately upon entering the room, I wash my hands. I then put on gloves. I have a choice of four kinds—with or without latex, with or without powder—and I ask the nurse what her personal favorite is, but she's cagey, so I just pick the ones that say "Vinyl examination gloves." They are uncomfortable. I am now also officially not allowed to kiss Kirsten on the lips. Feh.

We get Kirsten settled in, we make jokes, we check out the view, the TV stations, and the food selection, and we sit there as a number of people file in—nutritionist, nurse, lady who gives the EKG. This is a weird experience because Kirsten has to strip to the waist to have the EKG, and of course I'm still sitting there, and, you know, she's my wife, it's not like I'm going to turn away from her breasts, and the technician is there, and she's seen it all before, and we are all just hanging out there (well, Kirsten is really hanging out, ha ha ha) acting like this is perfectly normal. Shit like this just happens all the time these days, and I guess it all contributes to this feeling vaguely dreamlike. I mean, if you woke up and said, "I dreamed I sat and watched while you sat there bare-breasted and some woman attached electrodes to you," your spouse would probably be like, "You fuckin' weirdo! What a weird dream!" Yep. She'd probably also say you were a perv, but there is nothing even vaguely arousing about this scene.

Anyway, I guess they eventually do rustle up a surgeon some-where, because this guy comes in and makes a point of telling us he's doing this while some other patient of his is being prepped for some kind of other surgery, like we give a shit. He asks me if I want to be there, and I say yes, and he kind of hesitates. I promise I won't scream or faint, a promise I am confident I can keep because of the lingering effects of the imperial stout, and then he hesitates again and finds some kind of tactful way of ask-ing Kirsten if she wants me there. "He should be here if he wants to be," she says, and in a global sense, of course, I'd rather be just about anywhere else right now, but I also feel very much like I want to be here for this.

They tilt Kirsten's bed to some strange feet-up head-down angle, and this has the effect of cutting off my view of the actual cutting and stitching, which I think is just as well. Kirsten and I are both a little slap-happy, so we are just kind of irreverent and silly the whole time, which the doc seems very disconcerted by at first, but then eventually seems to warm up to. I mean, you know they are irreverent and silly about all this stuff when they get behind closed doors. How could you spend all day cutting into people and not be? So, for example, when he whips out this little plastic tub full of iodine with a red-handled sponge, I go, "Hey! No fair! He's got dunkaroos!"

Kirsten looks at the tub with the red handle and says, "Hey, are you going to spread Cheez Whiz with that?" and the guy just has no response. I guess mocking the surgical equipment and procedure might change the power dynamic for these people in a way that makes them uncomfortable. So they cover Kirsten in a plastic shroud and shove some wires into her chest, and then shove some plastic tubing into her chest, and then remove the wires and sew up the opening, and I just sit there watching this like it's all normal. When Kirsten finally sits up, she's got a four-way hose sticking out of her chest. This is the hose they will use to pump her full of at least four different kinds of medicine in the next few days.

Once the bedside surgery is over, it's time for me to go pick up Rowen, so I give Kirsten a hug but no kiss, strip off my gloves, and head off through the airlock.

A Cold Night in Hell

So while I've blown off parents' night at my own school I do make it to parents' night at Rowen's school. I am in a kind of daze even though the imperial stout has finally worn off. Rowen and her classmates perform a version of "The Three Billy Goats Gruff," which has been the focus of a lot of activity at her school for the past few weeks, which seems kind of ironic to me because we got ahold of a version of this story, about three goats who want to get across a bridge but are hindered by the evil troll who lives below, right about the time we wanted to move to a new place but were hindered by the evil troll who lived below, and thus we christened the Troll after the troll in this story.

The play is short and predictably cute. Rowen plays the water under the bridge (when you have fifteen kids and a four-character story, you have to stretch a little), and she does a good job. I'm impressed because she is terribly shy, and the last time they had one of these events she refused to get off of Kirsten's lap. The kids all sing three songs, and Rowen refuses to get off my lap for this part, but she is singing. Afterward there is a potluck dinner. I, like a lot of the other parents, want to be social, but I just can't. Rowen and I kind of huddle by ourselves while we eat and are joined by the seven-year-old sister of one of her classmates. She is very nice to both of us and talks about why she likes her school and clues us in to the fact that her dad has brought these amazingly delicious dessert items, and again I guess I have to wonder about God intervening. On this night when I just can't deal with talking to grown-ups, I find this gregarious kid in my path who makes this dinner a real pleasure for both of us.

I go home and get Rowen to bed, and my friend Scott comes over with pizza and beer, which I consume joylessly because I am so blitzed out, and at about 9:30 I start to feel chilly and check the thermostat and find that the temperature is 6 degrees lower than the thermostat setting. This is not something working furnaces allow to happen. I head down to the basement, flashlight in one hand, box of matches in the other, and if dining with a nice kid felt like God sort of patting me on the back, coming home after taking my wife to the hospital and having my furnace break when it's 20 fucking degrees outside feels like God kicking me in the nuts.

For a little background, the furnaces have been the curse of this building. Since we bought the house, each of the three furnaces has broken, in numerical order, so now it is unit three's turn. Each breakage has required at least two visits from the heating people. I have stopped calling the twenty-four-hour emergency line in the off-hours (when, for some reason, each of these things has been discovered) because I found out that what these guys do is charge you two hundred bucks to come out at nine o'clock and tell you that they don't have the part they need on the truck, and you really should schedule a service call tomorrow. The sad part is that it took me three of these visits to finally see the pattern. I have learned a little bit about furnaces from all this. I know now what a thermocouple is. I also know something to try when your pilot light has gone out and you relight it and your furnace starts sputtering with flames licking back toward the gas pipe in a really alarming way. I try it, and it doesn't stop the sputtering. Last time this happened I was told that I could run the furnace like this for a while, but, you know, don't go to sleep while it's doing that, so I run it long enough to make up the missing 6 degrees and then shut it down, hoping the house will hold the heat overnight.

I wake up in the middle of the night stressed out, cold, and alone.

Bubble Vision

After a few days in the bubble, the days start to run together for Kirsten. The same thing happens to me. I go over to the hospital every day, but it gets harder and harder to remember if something happened yesterday or the day before, or even the day before that.

One thing that happens is that my glove selection grows smaller and smaller. On the first day there were four kinds of gloves, and by day six we are down to two. I have been experimenting, and I find that the powder-free gloves totally suck, because they are incredibly hard to get on your hands, and, once on, they give you that sticky, thighs-on-the-hot-car-seat feeling, only on your hands. On day six, my only options are the vinyl powdered gloves and these horrible blue powder-free gloves, which is really no choice at all. I mean, blue! What am I, a Smurf?

Kirsten gets progressively worse for the first few days. She is hooked up to four different pumps which feed into the four-way hose implanted in her chest. She sleeps a lot. A couple of times when I see her, she kicks me out after a short time because she needs to rest. On day three, she starts to puke. They have her on a number of antinausea drugs, but the medicine is too strong, and she pukes everything up and then pukes up bile. I am there for one of these episodes and I hold the pink plastic bucket and rub her back as she hunches over, green liquid dribbling out of her mouth. It is gross, but more than that, it's just sad. She has never been sick from the cancer, but now they are killing her. I mean, they are literally killing her. It is really strange to realize that without major medical intervention (the stem cell transplant), the dose of medicine they are giving her is fatal. I realize that what I am watching is my wife dying. And then, I guess, thanks to the transplant, she will come back to life. So that she won't die from the disease that's not making her sick. This whole thing is just so incredibly bizarre.

On the second day I go to the hospital, I feel a big cry coming on. I am just so sad, but I have not broken down yet. Probably because there has just been too much to do—call to get the furnace fixed, get my mom settled in, teach my classes, go to the hospital, make dinner—I haven't had time to get as sad as I know I need to get. I even packed the Prince greatest hits CD with "Purple Rain" on it, which is a song that, in times of high stress, never fails to move me to tears, but all I get today is a dribble, even out of the part near the end where he is going "ooo— oooweoo-oooo-ooweeeoo-ooo-oo-oo" in that crazy falsetto, which is usually where I lose it.

Now I am walking down the street going to the hospital, and

I feel like I am about to sob. So I do what I have done so much since this started—I call Danny, who has been my best friend since the seventh grade. We lived two blocks from each other for about five years as adults, and—well, saying what he means to me is probably another book in itself, so I call him up, and I tell him I need some help getting my game face on, because I am going in to see Kirsten and I can't be this sad, I have to be up-beat, but they're killing her for God's sake, and I can't remember what exactly he says to me, but I know that it involves mocking me in some way, and it works perfectly. I think later on that he is the only person apart from Kirsten who would dare to mock me when I am sad, and the only person apart from Kirsten who could possibly know that that is the best thing he could do for me. I am lucky to have him.

The days all start to run together. Some days we have con-versations where I tell her about my day and she tells me about why she didn't sleep and makes fun of the medical staff. Some days she is really sleepy, and she says, "I'm sorry I'm not very good company," and I hold her hand for a while until she says, "I'm sorry, hon, but you have to leave so I can sleep." I bring her videos of Rowen and of people at church saying hi. She is puk-ing pretty much nonstop through the church video, which is no reflection on the lovely people there or their nice and heartfelt greetings, but she does seem to appreciate it. She raises her head long enough to sort of see who's talking, then hunches over her little puke bucket while they talk. The sound is bad anyway, so not much is lost. One day we have a hilarious time because she is high on Ativan, which is something they are giving her for her nausea but which is also, I guess, some kind of narcotic, and I am high on lack of sleep and caffeine. I can't remember the conversation, and I know she doesn't either, but I just remember both of us sitting there and laughing a lot. Some days I feel good about what's happening, and some days I feel horrible. I am not used to being able to see her for only forty-five minutes a day. Mostly I just miss her.

Backstory

Kirsten and I have not been separated like this in twelve years. It sucked then, and it sucks now, but then it was also kind of fun in a romantic longing kind of way; now it just sucks.

We met as sophomores in college. We both lived in this Modern Language dorm, which I know sounds freakish, and I guess it kind of was, but I really loved it there because it was where I finally found the weirdos at this big school. My freshman year I lived on a hall where, but for the would-be Scientologist who tried to get his tuition refunded so he could run away to be reeducated or something, I was the weirdest person there. I am much more comfortable being the normal person among weirdos than the weirdo among normal people, so I was at home in the Modern Language House.

The dorm was unremarkable except that it had this really cushy, nice lounge with a kitchen, comfy furniture, and this kind of solarium deal. It was a great place to hang out, and Kirsten and I did a lot of hanging out that year. We, along with five or six other people, came to call ourselves "the lounge rats," because we were just there all the time. There were many Saturdays when everyone would kind of stagger down there at like 10:00 A.M., sit around and shoot the shit for a couple of hours, talk about how we all had work we needed to do (sometimes if somebody really felt the need to pretend they were going to study, they would bring books that they never opened), drift out at about noon to get sandwiches or make mac and cheese in the kitchen, drift back with food and say Okay, after lunch I am absolutely starting my work, and then sit around shooting the shit until around dinnertime, when we would frequently find ourselves so lazy that we would get a pizza delivered from the pizza place we could see right across the street and endure the disgusted looks of the delivery guys rather than get off our lazy asses. It was really great.

Although Kirsten and I spent hours in each other's company, we never spent any time together outside of this group, so in a strange way we didn't know each other that well, and we did not become a couple right away. I actually ended up dating a non-lounge-rat woman that year. Well, "dating" is not exactly the right word. I mean, we did go on some dates, but it was a college relationship, so what we mostly did was have enthusiastic, inexpert sex in those tiny, uncomfortable dorm beds. I should say in fairness that I am speaking only of myself when I say "inexpert," because I was a virgin before this and had an endurance of about twenty seconds, and when I think about it I guess that means I can really only speak for myself when I say "enthusiastic" too.

Anyway, this woman was actually dating some guy who had gone away for a semester abroad, so I was the Other Man. Which ended up hurting, because I wanted her to pick me, but she told me from the beginning that she wouldn't, and because I was an idiot I thought we were in love, and because she wasn't she knew that we had fun together and shared a mutual attraction and that was about it, but it took me years to realize that I resented her for not believing the lies I told myself about our relationship, and that she was right and I was wrong and I caused myself a lot of grief wanting this relationship to be something it wasn't.

The only real negative implication of this is that over the summer after all this ended, my ex-girlfriend from high school came over and just threw herself at me, but she was also dating somebody else, and since I was tired of being somebody's piece on the side, I pretended that I didn't get that she was throwing herself at me. I know that it was the right thing to do, but I still sort of regret it. How pathetic is that?

Kirsten and I finally spent some time alone together at the end of that school year, when we were both getting our paperwork together for our junior year in the U.K. We went and got passport pictures taken, picked up forms, and stuff like that. It was all aboveboard and totally nonromantic, but I felt vaguely guilty because I was "dating" somebody else and this felt kind of like a date. We then kept in touch over the summer—she lived in Boston and I lived in Cincinnati—and later that summer her sister, Nan, got married and moved to Cincinnati, and so Kirsten came to visit her, and this happened to coincide with my friend Rick's big polka party that he had been planning for weeks, so I suggested that she come along, and she agreed.

Now when I say polka party, it was just a party where Rick was playing a lot of polka music, it's not like there were actual accordions or anything. I don't remember much about the party except that Kirsten and I did flirty stuff like throw ice at each other, and that one of Rick's friends was hitting on Kirsten and I found myself getting totally jealous, and I hated this guy for years because of this, and Rick would say stuff like, "But he's a really nice guy!" and I'd be like, "He was hitting on my wife!" and Rick would sensibly reply that she wasn't even my girlfriend, much less my wife at the time, and eventually I did hang out with this guy again and found that Rick was right about him. An interesting postscript is that after we left, the cops showed up with this decibel-o-meter and gave Rick a ticket for violating the noise ordinance, but he decided to go in front of a judge for some reason, and when the judge heard that it was polka music, she laughed and dismissed the case.

Anyway, both Kirsten and I headed to the U.K. for our junior year—she to London and me to Edinburgh. We wrote letters a lot, and once she came up to visit and we went to the movies and then to a pub and came back to my room, and something was on the verge of happening, I mean I was about thirty seconds away from going for the awkward first kiss, when my friend Hugh burst into my room drunk off his ass and planted himself for a good hour. That pretty well killed the moment, so nothing happened that night, but now I was thinking about her all the time. When Christmas break came, I went to London for the first week, and I just remember thinking that it was too much for me, I had to say something. So at one point we were out walking around London and I ended up picking her up, I mean literally lifting her off her feet under some pretext I no longer remember, so I was holding her around the waist and I said something smooth like, "So what's going on with us anyway?" and she replied something equally smooth like, "I dunno," but we decided that something was happening, and I remember the first time we kissed we were standing outside the British Museum, and for the whole rest of the week we held hands and kissed constantly, and it was just wonderful.

We saw each other at least twice a month for the rest of the year, and wrote each other letters daily. I took the eight-hour bus ride from Edinburgh to London what seemed like a hundred times, and you can tell how in love I was by the fact that I came to love those bus rides. They were full of romantic anticipation, and even now if I saw the bus station in Edinburgh I would probably well up, because the bus meant Kirsten, and even eight hours on the bus was painless because she was waiting at the other end.

We called each other a lot, and this was frustrating, because in my dorm the phone was down the hall and through a door, and hardly anybody ever heard it ring, and in Kirsten's dorm there were three phones for the entire dorm, so I had to depend on the goodwill of some sullen person who was trying to watch their Australian soap opera in the lounge next door to answer the phone and then page Kirsten on the PA. Then I would wait a long time for her to get downstairs if she was there, and wait even longer if she wasn't there, while the minutes were ticking off my phone card.

Anyway, we did the best we could to stay in constant contact, and we saw each other a lot and drank a lot and kissed a lot and had sex a lot, and after we came back we were pretty much inseparable—we both lived in the Modern Language House again as seniors, and we went to Taiwan for six months after graduation and then moved in together right after that. We had shitty first jobs and a shitty first apartment together, learned to cook together, got married, had a kid together, and basically I went from being a kid to being an adult with her, and when I say I don't know who I am without her it's because we have been together as I have become everything—husband, parent, teacher—that makes me who I think I am right now, and as I sit here writing this she is in the hospital and I miss her so much I can't stand it. I literally think the last time I spent this long without sleeping next to her was the summer after that junior year abroad, and it sucked then, but it sucks a whole lot more now.

Nobody Likes a Smartass

One day I bring in and hang up Christmas lights in Kirsten's hospital room. I do such a crappy job that they all fall down in the night, and Kirsten's dad does it right the following day. He also brings in a sign that Kirsten and I have been talking about since day one. She has this window that faces the corridor, and she can never really leave the room, so we decide that she needs a sign that says, "Please Do Not Tap on the Glass. It Disturbs the Animals." She gets her dad to make it because he is the master of clip art, and she wants little pictures of zoo animals surrounding the words. One day I go in and it is hanging up. I think this may be the only positive thing about this whole experience—who's going to tell her to take it down? Who would dare? They may or may not find it funny (not, in most cases—as I have noted, irreverence just doesn't seem to play very well with medical types), but they damn sure aren't going to take it down. A few days later in a similar spirit, I steal a bunch of stickers from her room. They are safety orange and say CHEMOTHERAPY in big black letters, and I have seen them stuck on the bags of crap they are pumping into her, but I stick one on my shirt, and I offer them around at work, and some people politely decline, some people give this nervous sort of "heh-heh" and say, "Uhhhh . . . I guess it's great that you're keeping your sense of humor, heh-heh," and sort of edge away from me uneasily. I think maybe only one or two people have any idea why I think this is a funny thing to do. I'm not really sure I do, but I think it's all about changing the power dynamic—not just between us and the medical people, but also between us and the treatment, us and the disease. In the hospital they take these stickers very seriously, as they have to, and I am glad they do because it helps everybody be damn sure which of the five bags hanging on Kirsten's incredibly heavy IV pole have the toxic substances in them, but the beautiful thing is that we don't have to take them seriously at all. Kirsten is planning to smuggle out a roll and then surreptitiously stick them on my teacups and stuff.

My mom used to tell me, "Nobody likes a smartass," and while it certainly seems true that the people where Kirsten is don't know what to make of her and the people where I am don't know what to make of me, we are completely on each other's wavelength. I think I can presume to speak for her when I say we both like at least one smartass.

Invasion of the Parents

Early in Kirsten's hospital stay, my mom moves in. It goes fine initially, but I'm nervous because the last time I spent any time at all with my mom was for a week last Christmas in Cincinnati. Kirsten, Rowen, and I had a great time. It felt like a very relaxing, laid-back visit. When we got home, however, I found that my mother wouldn't speak to me for three weeks. She later explained, in a letter, that she was heartsick because she felt that we were shutting her out. I had no fucking idea what she was talking about. She was mad about the fact, for example, that when she said she would baby-sit so we could go to the movies, we went to the movies and came home without staying out for five hours so she could bond with Rowen.

I remain baffled by this, but when I have grandchildren I know I will come to understand and that it will suck. So I am nervous about what this visit is going to bring. I guess I lied when I said that my mom doesn't have any long-simmering resentments, because ever since Rowen was born, there has been this tension about why do we live in Boston, why don't we come to Cincinnati more (mostly because it costs a hell of a lot less to fly one person out here than three people out there).

My mom has developed a story that explains all this. It goes like this: she always encouraged me to be independent, and then I spread my wings and flew away forever. This is a partial version of the truth, but it leaves out the fact that we got on each other's nerves to a shocking degree when I came home for summers in college—basically we just couldn't figure out how to be adults in that house together, so she acted like I was fourteen and so did I. Also, as I've said, we weren't really too connected to my mom's extended family when I was growing up, and we didn't belong to a church or anything that would sort of anchor me to the community, and the only thing larger than our two-person nuclear family that I felt connected to was my group of friends. And of all of them, only one still lives in Cincinnati, and even he's moving.

So the story is just more complicated than I am this independent kid who flew away. I mean, I did fly from the nest, but, you know, I was also pushed. Okay. The corollary story is that I am unreasonably exasperated with her. Now any adult with living parents can tell you that parents are just annoying. I mean, they are wonderful, and they gave us life, and I am mindful of the fact that I am here bitching about the people who are making it possible for me to continue to live my life at all while Kirsten is in the hospital, but the fact is that they are also just annoying. I do not mean this specifically about my mom, or Kirsten's parents. I do not know any adult who does not find their parents occasionally exasperating. And yes, I am fully, poignantly aware that I will one day be annoying to Rowen, and I hope that my mom is still around when that day comes so she can point at me and say, "See? Adult kids are just a pain in the ass! They never listen to your advice and they get all huffy if you so much as put a plate in the wrong place or make a simple suggestion about how they might do something differently with their kid, but they don't want to hear about your parenting experience, even though you obviously did a good job, just look how they turned out . . ."

One night while my mom is here, Kirsten's parents come over to take us all out for dinner to this really good pizza place, which is almost ruined by the melancholy folk stylings of this John Hiatt wannabe guy singing and playing guitar. The story of me as independent wing-spreader who doesn't sufficiently appreciate his mom and is unreasonably exasperated by her just becomes too powerful when there are three of them and one of me. Now I know how they feel when it's just one of them and two of us—they must hate it. I am sure we assert the story of them as meddling and occasionally feeble in a way that one of them can't fight.

I am so freaked out by all this that I run to the bathroom and call Kirsten on the cell phone. I don't really have anything to say, and I get a funny look from some guy who comes in to pee, and I'm sure he went right back to his table and said, "Some jackass is on a cell phone in the fucking bathroom talking about nothing!" but it is enough for me to just hear her voice. I feel better, and the melancholy folk singer slips in a Hank Williams tune amongst the many numbers by obscure depressive singer-songwriters, and I am pacified. Also the pizza is good.

Is God Listening?

One day after I visit Kirsten, I find myself stuck waiting for the elevators, a situation that annoys me to no end. There are three elevators and ten floors, but you can literally wait ten minutes for an elevator. They have machines in this hospital that can detect a cancerous spot on your spine only a few millimeters wide, but they can't seem to get people from floor to floor efficiently. I guess if they have to skimp somewhere, better on the elevators than on the life-saving equipment.

A woman is there, standing with me, waiting for the elevator, and we are both nervously checking our watches, because I have to get back to work for a meeting and she, as it turns out, is ten minutes over on her parking meter, and I say something lame like, "Boy, these are the slowest elevators in the world," and she says, "Yeah, we've been here for three weeks, and I still can't believe these elevators."

We are right outside the transplant unit, and three weeks is Kirsten's scheduled stay in the bubble, so I say, "Oh, do you have somebody in for a transplant?" and she says, "No, you wouldn't believe me if I told you."

Well, we're obviously going to be here for a while, so I indicate that she should tell me and then we'll see if I believe her, and she tells me that her sister-in-law came in to give birth, and something went horribly wrong, and they lost the baby, a ten-pounder, and the sister-in-law has basically been in a coma ever since, during which time she had four surgeries and dialysis, and she only just woke up today, and nobody's told her she lost the baby yet.

All I can think is "fuuuuuuuuuuuuuuuuck." What I say is, "Well, thank God she's alive," and I mean it—I think about the horror of that experience for the dad, and how awful it would be to go into the hospital for what you think is a happy occasion and then have your whole fucking family die, and so thank God that she didn't. The words fall out of my mouth before I have a chance to intellectualize, and it really feels like a prayer to me when I say it, because it comes from a much deeper place than my stupid conversational gambit about the elevators.

"Yeah," the lady says, "we've all been praying for her, and it worked!" and I envy this woman her certainty as we say goodbye, and later on I think, Well, presumably the people who are praying for her now were also praying for her to have a healthy baby. So how can you say it works?

I know her response would probably be to point to the success of the mother's survival and ask how I could say it doesn't. And I know I am asking the wrong question, or something. Faith isn't scientific, and here I am trying to examine data and make it fit the hypothesis, like life is a lab report for my creepy eighth-grade science teacher, or my perverted tenth-grade science teacher, or my foxy eleventh-grade science teacher. Or something.

So does it work? When Kirsten got good news from her second round of chemo, my mom told me that she thought everybody's prayers were helping, and how somebody she works with that Kirsten and I have never even met has these two sons who every night when they say their prayers before bed say,

"Please make Kirsten's medicine work." I am incredibly touched by this—I mean I am sitting here getting teary just thinking about it. I asked my co-workers to pray for us, and I asked my prayer group to pray for us, and I love it when we are in church and the minister says in the prayer something like, "We pray for those going through chemotherapy," or "We remember those waiting for test results," or something like that.

But God just can't get off that easy. I mean, if God made the second round of chemo work, he presumably made the first round not work, right? He presumably gave her cancer in the first place, right? He presumably killed that baby. And then something good happens and we go, "Thank God." Well, shit. I can't make sense of it, and I want so much to be one of those people who believe, I mean really believe deep in their souls, in God's goodness and justice, but I just can't square it with the data, and I know that's the wrong way to look at it, but I can't seem to make myself look at it any other way.

My sort of nebulous Christianity doesn't really offer much in the way of answers. When Job, sitting in shit and covered in weeping sores, asks, "Why me?" God doesn't offer that Job was the object of a wager between him and Satan, he just says, basically, Who the hell are you to ask me that? Shut the fuck up. Go make a universe, and then you can ask me about what goes on in mine.

Fair enough, I guess, but it sure isn't satisfying. One of those Christian heresies that caused lots of people to get persecuted and executed in the Middle Ages held that the universe was actually the object of an endless war between an equally powerful God and Satan. Now *that's* an explanation I could buy! God gets the credit, Satan gets the blame! And they killed people for believing this! Now people who believe this just get TV shows and control of the Republican party.

Sigh. I have prayed less since this whole thing started than at any time in the past year and a half. I just don't know what I'm doing, and I really wish I had the faith of those little kids, or the lady by the elevators, or my mom, or pretty much anybody.

Gotta Catch 'Em All

One day I head down the hall on the bubble floor, and I notice that there is a new sign on one of the other patients' doors. It says, "Please check with nurses before visiting pt." I don't know jack about what goes on on this floor, but this looks to me like it can't be good news. There are a bunch of people standing around the bed looking sad, and all I can think is that this person is dying.

They have their TV on and as I walk by I see this ad for the new gold and silver Game Boys, which in some way that I don't understand correspond to some new Pokémon games or something. And it just freaks me out. What must it be like to be dying and have fucking Pokémon ads playing on your TV? It seems absurd and obscene and kind of sad to me—like if someone is dying their TV ought to only show really meaningful stuff or something. What could it possibly be like to watch this commercial and think to yourself, "This is one of the last things I will ever see"? It strikes me as incredibly depressing. Then it occurs to me that perhaps it is a blessing. Maybe you can look at this dumbshit ad and go, "Well, there's nothing really left for me to stay for here," and just ease on over to the other side.

The Home Front

Rowen is not freaking out. Mostly. This is very good news. In the first few days that Kirsten is in the hospital, she cries a few times—once when I pick her up from school, we are just walking down the street and she starts to sob. I know the feeling. But she bounces back pretty quickly, and acts mostly like her normal self, which is to say that she is sometimes angelic and sometimes completely psychotic, which I guess is pretty standard preschooler behavior. A couple of weird things are that she starts refusing to talk to Kirsten on the phone, which is kind of odd because she has never been shy about the phone before, and she never wants me to tell Kirsten anything that happens at home. For example, I will be videotaping to show her the Christmas tree, and Rowen will say, "NO! Don't show her! Don't tell her!" I finally decide that this is about her wanting to be able to tell Kirsten everything when she gets home.

Rowen has this system of affection where she has number one, which has always been Kirsten, and number two, which is not exactly a close second, and that's me. I don't mean to suggest that she doesn't love me as much or anything. As I've said, we have a lot of fun together, but if it's a choice between me and Kirsten, she'll always choose Kirsten.

I have been waiting patiently for the change in positions that everyone says is inevitable, that eventually little girls are supposed to favor their dads, but she's almost four and it hasn't happened yet, so I have pretty much resigned myself to having to wait for her teenage years when that weird mother-daughter tension creeps in and dad reaps the benefits. If, that is, dad can restrain himself from being overprotective and never wanting his little angel to have a date with some wispy-mustached perv of a teenaged boy. Ahem. But some have greatness thrust upon them, and in Kirsten's absence I have taken over the number one spot. One day I tell Kirsten in the hospital, "I never wanted it like this!" I feel like the understudy who steps into the starring role because the star met with some kind of horrible accident.

And I don't know why this surprises me, but being number one is somewhat of a mixed bag. It is nice, sure, but it is also kind of exhausting, as it involves a fair amount of clinging. And while I love Rowen and it makes me feel needed and important, which is something I think everybody craves (I know it's something my mom craves, and the fact that she hasn't gotten it much from us since Rowen was born is probably key to a lot of the tension between us), at the same time, you know, sometimes you want, for example, to be able to be at church and go pee by yourself.

Now that I am number one, my mom moves into the number two spot for Rowen, which is good, I mean this is probably two spots higher than she's ever been in the affection hierarchy, but it is tough for her because being number two involves a lot of "NO! I want daddy!" and I know from personal experience that it's hard to take, but I do manage to convince my mom not to take it personally, that this is just the way Rowen is. Rowen apparently throws a couple of screaming fits in the morning, and this to me indicates that my mom has really arrived in Rowen's mind, because she will really only throw screaming fits at us and is totally silent for people she doesn't know or especially like.

It is helpful and nice having my mom here. I am initially annoyed by stuff like her using the oven as a drying rack for pots and pans (I ask her not to do it and then yell at her when, a few days later, I am preheating the oven and have to pull two pots with handles that miraculously hadn't melted yet out of the hot oven before sticking the food in) and the fact that she has a really terrible sense of direction (on the first night she complained about getting turned around in our house, which has five rooms). Mostly, though, my mom is pretty easy to hang around with, and we have a fairly decent time. I am reminded that I really don't appreciate her enough one night when Joe comes over to go out after Rowen goes to bed, and Rowen's bedtime is happening a little later than planned, so I leave Joe with my mom for a 'few minutes while I finish up the bedtime ritual, and as we are walking down the street later, I am about to apologize for abandoning him with my mom—not that my mom is so heinous or anything, but I think if I went to a friend's house and was forced into conversation with their mom I had never met before it would feel pretty awkward—but before I can open my mouth, Joe says, "I really enjoyed talking to your mom! She's really cool." He's right, and I feel guilty for thinking I needed to apologize.

One night she is watching TV, and I come in to join her and she is watching *Providence,* and I say, because I've never watched it, "Oh, is this any good?" because she tends to favor the "Quality TV" kind of TV, whereas I like to watch cartoons and rich people throwing stuff at each other, and she says, "No, not really." And I say, "But you watch it regularly," and she says, "Yeah. I just really can't explain it." It baffles me, but I do sit down and watch the entire episode, and it is corny, cheesy, and unbelievable—a total throwback to those hero-doctor shows of the 1970s, except starring this really attractive woman with great hair. In fact, between her great hair and Mike Farrell's white hair, which just makes me go, "BJ! You're so old!" because of course I grew up on *M*A*S*H* in the BJ years, the show is really all about hair as far as I'm concerned.

Even though the show is awful, it is somehow a nice evening.

Cry If I Want To

Two Sundays before Christmas we have this fully packed day. We go to church and Rowen is going to be in the Christmas pageant as a sheep. This is what passes for a rite of passage among Unitarians—you start as a sheep, then move up to angel, then to townsperson, then, if you are lucky, to Three King or holy family. So Rowen is beginning her journey, and after one practice during church school we hear that she was the best sheep in the place, but then when it comes time to practice it in the church in front of people, she starts sobbing: "I don't wanna go up there without you! I'm scaaaared!" So, in another Unitarian rite of passage, I take over the role of father ram from another parent who has played the role for three years.

I have brought Joe and Katy's camcorder to record the event, but now I have to be up there, and I can't really be taping it then, so I hand the camcorder over to my mom and explain that it's very simple to operate, basically just point and shoot, and I should know that we are in for trouble when she looks in the wrong end and says, "I don't see anything." But okay, I figure it's no big deal, if the camcorder is in my mom's hands, I have a small but greater than zero chance of getting the event taped, and if it's just sitting in a pew, there is pretty much zero chance that it's going to tape the pageant on its own.

The pageant goes okay and afterward we go to coffee hour in the parish hall and grab a snack, and my mom just disappears. I spend about ten minutes looking for her—I stand on the stage and scan the crowd and try to be polite to the nice people who come to talk to me without really looking at them, because then I won't be able to see her, and eventually I see her and smile and wave.

Rowen and I go over to her, and I see that she has tears in her eyes. I am convinced that she thinks I blew her off, because this is kind of a theme in our relationship, so I immediately say, "I've been looking and looking for you, and I couldn't find you," so as to make the point that I didn't just ditch her.

Well, I don't know why I am still learning this lesson after thirty-two years, but it is folly trying to read my mom's mind, because when she gets home, she starts crying full-on and says how she couldn't work the camcorder and she felt like that ruined the experience of the pageant for her, and she is never here to see these kinds of things, and she had bought this new outfit for Rowen that doesn't fit, and she wanted to brush Rowen's hair but I wouldn't let her, and now Rowen looks like hell.

I am explicitly indicted on the last count, because my mom has been sort of obsessively trying to brush Rowen's unruly hair all the time and I told her that Rowen's routines are very important to her and now was not the greatest time to be adding new ones. I am implicitly indicted on the other two counts because I am the one who gave her the camcorder and, okay, perhaps unreasonably expected her to be able to work it, and I rushed her out of the store when we were buying Rowen's outfit because it was late and it was full of insane Christmas shoppers and I felt like screaming.

I apologize to her, but I am mad. I am mad because she said that Rowen looked like hell while Rowen is sitting right there, but most of all I am mad because I just don't have the energy to deal with this right now. My wife is in the hospital, I have to worry about how my daughter is feeling, and I just don't have the time or energy to worry about taking care of my mom's feelings. Perhaps that makes me an asshole. I don't know. All I do know is that I am so fucking tired that it's all I can do to take proper care of myself.

I also think, well, here we go again. Every visit these days seems to involve tears, and it always seems to boil down to me being a bad son in some way, and while this is difficult to deal with at any time, right now it is enough to just send me to bed.

My mom calms down, and Rowen and I head off to the fourth birthday party of one of her classmates. It is, without exception, the coolest birthday party I have ever attended, including adult ones. They have rented out this club which is under a pizza place and is like half club, half bowling alley. They have this jukebox stocked full of CDs by the knowledgeable guys who run the record store next door, and I feed it dollars and play "I Want You Back," "Pressure Drop," "I Say a Little Prayer" (the Aretha Franklin version), and "It's Not Unusual." Other people make good selections too—it's tough not to when there are so few bad CDs on offer—and I am just delighted.

I must take a detour here and say that one of the CDs they have stocked is the first Devo album (*Q: Are We Not Men? A: We Are Devo!*), and as I am flipping through I see it and remember that it has a song called "Mongoloid" on it. We kind of thought that was funny when we were twelve listening to it at Danny's house, and I say this as a Devo fan, but it is a cruel and shitty song. There is a kid at this party with Down's syndrome, and I now know enough about living through tough situations that I am not going to say that her mom is a hero or that the girl is this perfect little angel or anything, because I'm sure her mom gets frustrated and I am sure that the kid is a pain in the ass sometimes as all kids are, but nevertheless, they are very loving, and the kid is just incredibly cute and sweet, and I just think how shitty it is that that fucking song is on the jukebox here. And I am horrified when, later, somebody from the other birthday party also taking place in this space actually plays it. I can only believe that they were oblivious to this girl's presence, because any other explanation is just too horrible to contemplate, but anyway, I look nervously at the mom, and she is totally oblivious, she's totally got the music tuned out, and I guess she's not familiar enough with the Devo oeuvre to recognize it.

If I were God, there would be hell to pay for that kind of insensitivity, and I would also make sure that every one of those plastic-helmeted motherfuckers in Devo had about five kids with Down's syndrome that they had to one day explain that song to.

But, you know, if I were God, I'd change a lot of things.

Anyway, with that one horrifying exception that happens at the end of the party, the music is cool, the kids are bowling and having fun, some of the adults have beers, and all of this is so unlike the usual kids' birthday party, where you usually stuff a whole bunch of kids into someone's house and play really horrible music and they all get squirrelly and overstimulated and everybody goes home a little crankier than when they came. We eat great pizza, not that cardboard shit that the chains throw in front of kids because they can get away with it. I like Rowen's classmates a lot, and I am in awe of this party.

And as we sit there and eat our pizza, I look at all these other happy families and I get this uncontrollable urge to cry. I run to the bathroom, and I stand there and just cry and cry. There is something about the fact that this party is so good that makes me miss Kirsten so much it almost physically hurts. Hell, it does physically hurt—it makes me cry in a way that I am unable to hold back. I want her here, enjoying this party with us. I want her back, as Michael Jackson said. Yeah yeah yeah yeah. Ooo-oo baby.

Out of the Mouths

Driving home from the party, we have to go by our old house. When we turn down the street, Rowen says, "Hey! We're not going to the old house! We're going to our new house!" and I say, "Yeah, but we have to go by the old house to get to the new house from here. Believe me, I don't even want to be on this street."

She digests that for a moment and says, "Why don't you like the old house? I liked it."

"Well," I say, "it's complicated. One day I'll explain the whole story of why we had to move." We have tried to protect her from the horrible reality of the Troll, especially since we don't really want her to know that it was her walking around that set him off, because God knows how that information could screw up a kid's mind.

She, however, is a smart kid and will not be put off. "You can tell me now," she says, and I come back with, "Well, there are a lot of reasons," still trying to stall, and she says, "Tell me what they are."

"Okay," I say. "Well, you know how three people owned that house, and we were one of the people? Well, it's just easier to make decisions and stuff when only one person owns the house, and we are the only ones who own our new house."

"Also"—I decide to go for it—"remember that guy who yelled at mommy?" And Rowen says, "No . . . ," which is nice, because we were convinced she was scarred for life by that whole incident, and I say, "You know, that guy who yelled at mommy in the driveway one morning when you were going to school?"

"Oh yeah!"

"Well, that guy was just not a nice guy, and he used to do stuff like yell like that, and we just didn't want to live around him anymore."

She digests that, then says, in this totally matter-of-fact, almost bored tone, "Well . . . I guess he'll probably yell at other people now."

I just start to laugh. "Roo," I say, "You are so right . . ." and I am still laughing, and she adds, "He will probably yell at the people who moved in after us," and all I can do is say, "Yes he will," and laugh some more.

I Got the Luck

My mom seems kind of contrite the day after her outburst. I come home from work and find the house filled with a delicious smell—she has made black bean soup, and it turns out to be surprisingly good. I gave up on black bean soup a few years ago because I just couldn't make it interesting, but hers has a little extra zing, which she reveals comes from a can of tomato sauce. Plus there is liquid smoke involved, and I love liquid smoke so much I could probably eat it over ice cream.

We have a very nice evening, and things seem back to normal—we are relaxed and enjoying each other's company, laughing and joking and generally having a pretty good time. She makes a couple of conversational salvos about yesterday— "Yesterday was a tough day for me" and suchlike things—but I don't take the bait because I don't want to ruin a nice evening with a Meaningful Talk.

The next day, Rowen and I are walking home from school holding hands, and she is in a really good mood. We are talking and laughing, and these are some of my favorite times, when the two of us are not really doing anything but enjoying each other's company. As we reach our street, out of nowhere she starts doing a little dance and chanting, "I got the luck! I got the luck! I got the luck!" (This bears a strong resemblance to her "I'm the bomb" chant and dance that she did a few weeks earlier.) I have no idea where this came from or exactly what it means, but I look at her smiling and jumping up and down on the sidewalk and I am just so full of love I could explode (and I know that's one of those sappy parent things to say, but it's really true), and I think about how I have this great little girl, and a cool mom I really love, and a wife I love more than anything, and my own cozy home, and even though Kirsten is in the hospital I feel really happy and blessed and I just start jumping up and down on the sidewalk with Rowen, the two of us going, "I got the luck! I got the luck! I got the luck!"

Kirsten, Baxter, Newt

"They finally got me a new pump," Kirsten announces over the phone. "I love it so much. I think I'm going to have to leave you for it." She has been agitating for a new pump basically ever since she got in here. She has had three or four things pumping into her at all times, and each substance has its own pump, and each pump hangs on this pole that is huge and sturdy, and Kirsten must wheel the entire thing, which probably weighs at least fifty pounds, with her every time she goes to the bathroom or gets out of bed, and it's a gigantic pain in the ass.

But now she has gotten one of the brand-new pumps that can pump three things at once. This is much lighter than three separate pumps, so it can be attached to a much lighter pole, and so it continues to be amazing what constitutes good news these days, but there you have it. I go and visit her and she is just elated. She still has to drag a pole with her everywhere she goes, but it is much easier than before, and it feels like a partial reprieve to her.

I look at the pump and notice that it's called the "Colleague 3" and I tell Kirsten that she really should have told me she was leaving me for a colleague. The company that makes the pump is called Baxter, so she says, "Yeah, his name is Baxter. He's been pumping me all morning."

We laugh, and then she says, "I'm sorry, but I just felt like I had to preempt you before you pulled a Gingrich on me." Newt, you may remember, the stalwart of the family values party, served his wife divorce papers while she was in the hospital undergoing treatment for cancer. And while I rolled my eyes at that factoid when I first heard it, now I really understand in my bones what a complete asshole you have to be to do something like that. And that makes me almost wish I believed what all the lunatics who loved that guy believe, because then I could at least take comfort in the knowledge that Satan is devising some really horrible punishment for him as we speak, but as it is I'll have to content myself with the knowledge that he is fat and out of a job, and if he would only lose his home and get addicted to crack and have to beg for change on the streets that might start to even things up as far as I'm concerned, but of course he is probably pulling down fat speaking fees and doing all the lucrative shit that failed politicians get to do, while, for example, the guy who wrote "96 Tears" is probably pushing a broom somewhere.

Anyway, I am in no danger of pulling a Gingrich. Kirsten's Baxter joke just reminds me again, not that I really need reminding, that I am lucky enough to have found the perfect woman for me, and how many people in their whole lives ever get to say that?

Cruel to Be Kind

I go over to see Kirsten one day, and after passing through the airlock, I see Dr. J. I spoke to Kirsten earlier, and she told me that she had gotten up in the middle of the night and almost passed out, and that in the morning the nurses were saying things like, "You really gave us a scare last night," and other such reassurances, so I ask Dr. J what happened. She is her usual friendly, upbeat self, and tells me that Kirsten has low blood pressure, once again using crystal-clear analogies (she compares blood pressure to a gas gauge, by way of explaining why they keep taking Kirsten's both standing up and lying down) and speaking in a methodical but not condescending way, and reassuring me. She is both incredibly knowledgeable and good at the people stuff, which, to judge by our encounters with everybody else, is basically unheard of in the medical profession.

I think once again about how lucky we are to have her on Kirsten's case. And then I think that it might not all have to do with luck. In some strange way, having Dr. J in charge of Kirsten's treatment is the result of some small nice thing I did years ago. Kirsten and I were on the membership committee at church, and one of the things we were working on was being more welcoming to newcomers. See, after church we have this coffee hour thing where everybody socializes, and the people at our church are, as I keep saying, these really nice, kind, caring people, but everybody just ignores the newcomers and they stand there, coffee in hand, with this pathetic "won't somebody please talk to me" look on their faces while all the nice, kind members of the church are running around talking to the other nice kind people and leaving these new people feeling like the kid who didn't get picked for the kickball team.

Now I have become one of those people who ignore newcomers, because I have to chase Rowen around, and I want to check in with the seven nice people that I only see on Sunday, and also I spend so much time in church school that I've had a few embarrassing conversations where I go, "So, are you new here?" and they answer, looking kind of annoyed, "Well, I've been coming for six months." But we met Dr. J pre-Rowen, and Kirsten and I remembered all too painfully how horrible it was to stand there at coffee hour feeling invisible because we did it for weeks, so we made it our mission to talk to people we didn't recognize, and one day I wasn't really feeling like it, because the fact is that these conversations frequently suck in the way that first conversations tend to: "So, do you live in the neighbor-hood? Oh. What do you do for a living?" Ack. It's an ironic feature of the Unitarian coffee hour that religion, which is, after all, the one thing you may have in common with someone you meet for the first time at a church, is never discussed. This is partly I think because Unitarians are so afraid of offending anybody that we welcome everybody with a vaguely religious leaning into the church, so you have Christians and Buddhists and even atheists (go figure) all coming to the same church, so talking about religion can open up a can of worms, but also I think it's that Unitarians tend to be college-educated liberals, and we are sort of embarrassed by our religiosity, like talking about God will immediately make us seem like one of those Bible-thumping, gay-hating, secretly-dating-a-hooker guys you see on TV.

Anyway, one morning I wasn't feeling like having any awk-ward conversations, but Kirsten poked me in the ribs until I went up to talk to this lady I didn't recognize, who turned out to be Dr. J. And as I mentioned, she was a "church friend" for years before she became Kirsten's doctor, and she always says that my saying hi to her that one morning was the reason she joined the church, because she was on like her third Sunday of standing there feeling stupid, and she said she had decided to never come back if someone didn't talk to her, and I did.

In the middle of all this shit, this horrible shit that has made me question just about everything I or anybody else believes, here is something good, something that makes sense: one day I did something nice, admittedly more out of a sense of duty than sheer friendliness, and also to stop the sharp pain in my ribs, but still, I did something nice, and as a result we have this incredibly bright and kind person in charge of the fight against Kirsten's cancer. It's kind of humbling, in a way—how often do we have opportunities to do some nice little thing, but we blow it off because nobody's elbowing us to do it?

I have an opportunity to find out a few days later. It's the last day before Christmas vacation, school is out, and I am running up the stairs to go get some free food, and I see one of my advisees on the stairs, and she has been having a real crisis lately, a really super hard time, a time as hard as or maybe harder than mine, and she says, "Oh, my bus pass!" just like that. And I get annoyed because she wasn't in advisory period to get her bus pass because she always spends advisory period with another advisor, and as stupid as it is, I think that must feed my sense of social insecurity, and I know that's pathetic—who's the seventeen-year-old here anyway? I am running up the stairs and she expects me to run back down into the basement without even bothering to ask me politely. So I say, "Yeah. Your bus pass is downstairs," and keep moving, and she gets mad and storms out of the building, and I immediately feel like a shit, remembering that I've just been shitty to a seventeen-year-old in crisis, and I have this vanity about having a good relationship with the kids, and what have I done here except shit on somebody a little lower down in the shit than me. What I said may not sound that bad, but it was—it was, and as a Unitarian I use this word carefully, a sin because I was deliberately cruel. I knew as I was saying it that I was going to piss her off. I'm like the little brother who kicks the dog because there are no people younger than me, and while I have been pretty proud of the way I've held it together during this whole thing, today I am ashamed of myself. One small act of kindness had big repercussions in my life. I can only hope that one small act of cruelty doesn't.

What You Need

My mom has a 6:00 A.M. flight, so she needs to get out early. We call for a cab the night before, and it's supposed to come at 4:45. Ugh. The plan is that she will sneak out and get into the cab and be on her way and not wake anybody else up. This is key for me, because Rowen had woken up at 4:30 the night before crying about being scared of monsters, and since it was after 5:00 by the time she got back to sleep, I never really got back to sleep, and the fact is that Rowen has woken up in the middle of the night scared of monsters for the last five nights in a row, which I guess is her way of dealing with the stress of missing her mom. I can't really complain, I mean her very attractive teacher told me the other day that they haven't noticed any change in her at all at school, which is good, because, you know, she's almost four, maybe she would start biting or throwing poop or other horrifying antisocial behavior. But she's not. She just wakes up crying every night. And this wears me out. When I finally do get an uninterrupted night's sleep a few nights later, I am amazed at how much difference it makes.

So I am a mess. I am getting through at school because I have taught this stuff before, but I am feeling guilty because I'm not really at the top of my game and since I am going to the hospital during all my free time, nothing is getting corrected, and the last week before vacation is tough under the best of circumstances, but it is wearing me down right now. Anyway, I hear my mom leaving, which is difficult to avoid given the fact that we live in five rooms and the door is right outside my bedroom. No problem. But then I wait to hear a little honk, or the heavy thunk of a cab door, and I don't. After several minutes, she comes up and goes to the bathroom and then goes back down the stairs. Minutes go by, and I still hear no thunk. I am clearly not going to get back to sleep until I satisfy my curiosity, so I throw some clothes on and head out into the hallway. I see my mom standing by the door. She says, "I may need to press you into service. They still haven't come." It is now 5:15, half an hour after the cab was supposed to come.

"Did you call them?" I ask. "No," she says, like it didn't even occur to her. Now it's not that driving her to the airport will be such a hassle—there won't be much traffic at this hour, and Kirsten's mom is also here to look after Rowen, but Jesus, how long was she going to wait before calling them? I get that annoyed "Why do I have to do everything?" feeling, and I call them and they say they will be here in five minutes. They haven't come after five minutes, so we go get in the car, and just as I am starting the car, the cab comes. I don't really feel like driving, and anyway I know the cab will bust all eight cylinders of his monstrous vehicle to get to the airport as fast as he can, so I put her into the cab and come back inside and lie in bed and don't sleep.

Later that day I am on my way to the hospital and I call to make sure she got in okay, and she did, and she tells me that my aunt Margie cleaned her entire house while she was gone, I am talking about scrubbing the kitchen, flowers on the table, the whole deal, and my mom is literally crying because she is so touched.

And I know this makes me a bad person, but it is all I can do to not say, voice dripping with sarcasm. "Yeah, it sure is nice to have someone take care of you, isn't it?" Or I guess maybe I'm not such a bad person because I don't end up saying every shitty thing that comes into my mind. I am aggravated because being taken care of is what I really want and need at this point. I am getting up in the middle of the night every night, I am running around trying to do everything, I am exhausted, and I just feel like I really would have liked to have someone take care of me. And my mom just can't. I mean, it's not like she did nothing, she did a lot of things—she hung our Christmas decorations, she took Rowen to school every day, she went grocery shopping, but the logistical support was not overwhelming the way that my aunt's scrubbing my mom's house was. Stuff got done at a maintenance level, which is admittedly more than I could have ever done on my own, but I never got that "Relax, I'll take care of everything" feeling from her. And I was keenly aware the whole time that my mom had this agenda about bonding with Rowen, and as her outburst showed, she can't really take care of me emotionally, so I just feel like a petulant little kid when I hear that someone has done this overwhelming nice thing for my mom, because that's what I want.

Not that I ever communicated this to her. And I realize this is exactly the reverse of what happened last Christmas. She had something she wanted out of that visit that she never told us, and she was mad when we didn't read her mind, and I complained that she was nuts, and it looks like I'm the one who's nuts now. It depresses me. It seems like we each want something that the other one can't give—I want her to take care of me, and she wants me to take care of her, and for whatever reason, we can't do that.

This naturally leads me to the fear that the same thing will happen to me and Rowen. I have been tap-dancing around some of the messier details of it all, but I think what's fucked up about my relationship with my mom all goes back to my dad's death. Or maybe not—I know plenty of people who have fucked-up relationships with their parents that haven't been informed by tragedy, so maybe my little analysis here is just so much bullshit, but here goes.

See, my mom went a little bit nuts after my dad died. And

I do not blame her for this one bit. When she was my age, she was already widowed a year, and she too had been with her spouse since she was a teenager, so I know exactly why it sent her over the edge. She ended up trying to have the rowdy adolescence or early-twentyhood experience that she never really got to have. And I should say here that she was never an addict, and we always had food, and, miraculously enough given the pitiful sums we lived on, I never felt poor as a child. Which I think may have had to do with some creative financing using credit cards, and my mom still has a problem with that that I sort of chide her for, but I never complained when I was actually getting Christmas presents when she was working for minimum wage. But anyway, she was gone a lot, partying with friends during my middle school years, and while it's certainly true that she always believed in me and encouraged me, maybe this is part of why I grew so independent. I know that she has tremendous guilt about this time, which I wish she wouldn't because if Kirsten dies I am heading straight up to the park to look for the crack dealers, or more likely I'll just start buying beer by the keg and suck from the tap until I can't feel anything anymore, but I wonder if she feels like my independence is this constant rebuke for those times and that's why it hurts so much.

What the hell do I know? Not much, except that we can't stop hurting each other's feelings. I hate it.

Santa Claus Is Back in Town

Because it is Christmastime, I start listening to a lot of Christmas music. Well, actually, I have only three Christmas albums that I put into heavy rotation: Elvis's Christmas album, which I don't really know the title of because I have all the songs as part of a box set, *A Christmas Gift for You from Phil Spector,* and the *Jackson 5 Christmas Album.* That's the order in which I listen to them, and I like rock and roll Christmas albums a lot more than sort of more traditional kinds of albums—I have a Sinatra Christmas album that I rarely listen to, and my mom used to always play the Barbra Streisand Christmas album, and what she does to "Jingle Bells" ought to be punishable by public flogging. Rock and roll Christmas albums do have a significant problem, though. This is that everybody figures they are going to write the next big Christmas standard by writing about how they want somebody who's far away to come home for Christmas, or how they want the estranged lover back for Christmas, or whatever. I initially forget about this and am therefore surprised to find myself moved by "Blue Christmas," which is a good song but has about as much genuine emotion as, say, an episode of *Providence,* and there is another song on the Elvis record called "Santa Bring My Baby Back to Me" that also catches me by surprise, but after a few listens I seem to be kind of inoculated against the whole thing, so that by the time I hit "Christmas (Baby Please Come Home)" on the Phil Spector album, I seem to be immune.

So I just enjoy the records. The thing I listen to the most on the Elvis CD is "Santa Claus Is Back in Town," which is a totally raunchy kind of R&B number in which the king basically boasts of his earning power and sexual prowess. There is one part that is just unbelievably raunchy where he instructs the listener to hang up her pretty stockings because Santa Claus is coming down her chi-him-ney tonight. I know what he's talking about. You hear a lot of these salacious double entendres in old songs like this, and I am stunned that they dared to put this on a Christmas album and a little sad that we don't seem to have much in the way of salacious double entendres in music these days. Much as I love Prince, a song like "Feel U Up," just to pick a random raunchy one, just doesn't pack the same clever punch as some of these old R&B numbers. I mean, comin' down your chimney. Honestly.

I then shift over to Phil Spector, and I am simply stunned by this record every year. I think it just might be one of the best pop records ever. Sure, the CD really reveals the limitations of the original recording—Phil's famous "Wall of Sound" sounds a lot more like a "55-Gallon Drum of Sound"—but the arrangements (actually done by Jack Nitzsche for a flat fee of fifty bucks) are just great. The "Santa Claus Is Coming to Town" arrangement is so great, in fact, that it was stolen by both Bruce Springsteen and the Jackson 5. Except for the shrill "Parade of the Wooden Soldiers," there really isn't a bad song on it—he even manages to make the creepy Oedipal fable "I Saw Mommy Kissing Santa Claus" kind of palatable. It ends with Phil ranting incoherently over a string arrangement of "Silent Night" about how much the album means to him, and he uses "so" and "very" about five times in each sentence. He comes across as such a freak on this track that it's sort of surprising that it took him another seventeen years to snap so badly that he pulled a gun on the Ramones.

The *Jackson 5 Christmas Album* is uneven but has two outstanding tracks: "Up on the Housetop," which I play over and over again because it just sounds like pure joy, and "The Little Drummer Boy," which is a song that always gets me anyway, but if you ever have a chance, you really need to hear what Michael Jackson does to this song. He sings it so well and really packs each "rum-pa-pum-pum" with emotion, and I am not talking about the kind of hysterical overemoting that passes for soul in Whitney Houston and Mariah Carey (and, sadly, latter-day Michael Jackson) songs, I am talking about understated but very moving singing. I am struck as I listen to it that he was just a little kid, and I would guess by the amount of horrible little kid singing you hear that this kind of thing is pretty much impossible to teach, and he really must be some kind of musical genius. So what the hell happened? How did he become the King of Tripe?

The other thing that strikes me as odd about this is that, as Jehovah's Witnesses, the Jacksons didn't celebrate Christmas, or at least they weren't supposed to. And yet this album is full of them talking about the stuff they want from Santa. As much as the songs are moving, they are basically a lie—one more cynical Christmas money grab. I have to wonder how this whole thing played down at the Kingdom Hall, and when I think about these kids in the recording studio feigning Christmas joy and then going home and being told that celebrating Christmas is a sin, it gets kind of easy to see how they're such fucked-up adults.

And speaking of fucked-up adults, that just about describes me. My Christmas spirit is about as fake as Jermaine Jackson's at this point. I am listening to the music, but it just isn't getting me into the spirit. Kids at school ask me what I want for Christmas, and I say, "My wife back," and they kind of don't know what to say, and I know it's a crappy thing to say to a teenager who is trying to make conversation, but it's true. I just don't give a shit about Christmas, and it's a damn good thing that Kirsten bought all of our presents before she went in the hospital, because I simply can't bring myself to shop. I am sort of reminded of the Kinks' song "Father Christmas" where the poor kids beat the shit out of Santa and take his money and basically say in that cynical Kinks way that Christmas is a luxury, and while I certainly have the money, I don't have the energy to care about this holiday, though I wish I could buy into the whole idea that it's a time of rebirth and hope. I do feel hopeful that they will save Kirsten's life—but mostly I just want to sleep for a week.

Driving over to the hospital one day, I hear "Do They Know It's Christmas," which I always liked much better than any of the other treacly benefit songs, because it at least has a little bit of an edge. Even in high school we thought about how many of the famine victims the song was about were not Christians, and how maybe "Do They Care It's Christmas" was a more appropriate question, but anyway, the line I am thinking of they give to Bono, who yowls, "Tonight thank God it's them instead of you," and while I do not claim to compare my fat ass to a famine victim, I also sort of feel like my family is a walking (or, in Kirsten's case, lying-in-bed) billboard for that sentiment at this time of year which is so very very special to so very many people, as Phil Spector might say.

Touch Me

After my mom takes off, I find that she's left behind one of those shower scrubby things, three earrings, and the new U2 album (which ironically enough is called *All That You Can't Leave Behind),* which she bought for herself but I quickly appropriate since she left it here. I have it in the CD player on my way to the hospital the day we get out for vacation. It's a really great record, and it's nice to see that they believe they can do what they're good at again and that they don't have to be some hyper-ironic techno band, or whatever the hell they were trying to be for the last five years. Everybody knows they don't have a sense of humor, and dammit, we like it that way.

So I am listening to it, and it is great but not exactly the cheeriest thing you've ever heard because it's about real adult topics like dying and stuff, which admittedly might not have been the best choice for me, but I'm listening to it anyway. I stop for lunch at this burrito place and read a little bit of a book my mom left behind, which is *Mystic River* by Dennis Lehane, which is a crime novel set in Boston, but it is also horribly depressing because it's about these people with horribly depressing dead-end lives and then somebody gets killed, and their shitty lives get even worse than they were before.

All of this is to say that I am not in the greatest mood on this particular day, and when I get to the hospital, I give Kirsten a hug, and I just start to cry. This is not because I am sad about the treatment or anything—she has been in the trough, but she is on the way up now, her counts are coming up and so are her spirits, and she is much less nauseous, so they don't have to give her Ativan and Benadryl anymore, so she seems much more like herself. It's just that the physical sensation of holding her feels like an electric shock. I just immediately feel throughout my body how much I miss her, how much it hurts all the time to not be able to touch her, and I get through most days without even realizing it, but then today, all of a sudden, it hurts so much I could cry. So I do.

Merry Motherfuckin Christmas

My first year of teaching, I had a rather difficult class, and one kid in this class was named Sun (he had a brother named Moon), and as Christmas break approached, Sun used to enter class every day—well, the days when he wasn't high—singing a little ditty that went like this: "MER-ry MOTHERf(glottal-stop)n CHRISTmas," and I would protest feebly, and he would argue that he didn't actually swear, and while this shows what an iron-fisted disciplinarian I am in the classroom, it has also been haunting me as Christmas approaches this year. I just hear this kid's voice and his singsong obscenity in my head whenever Christmas comes up.

I am convinced it's going to be easy. Though I have been listening to the music, I have not been getting myself psyched up for the holiday or anything—what I'm most looking forward to is a little bit of extra sleep. As the vacation begins, Kirsten's folks take Rowen for a day, and I end up going out with my friend Petey to see *Crouching Tiger, Hidden Dragon,* which is, well, it's getting rave reviews, most of which seem to be coming from non-kung-fu fans who think it's really cool that they fight on wires in this movie, and it is really cool, but at the same time it's nothing I haven't seen in twenty other movies, and plus, the director, Ang Lee, has brought a little too much *Sense and Sensibility* to this, if you ask me. There are many scenes with people sitting around talking in beautiful settings, and that's fine, but actually I want to watch these people kicking each other's asses a little more and talking about the nature of fate a little less. I have been contemplating the nature of fate plenty lately—what I haven't done is kicked the shit out of any old enemies, and that's what I came to the movies to see. The movie is half an hour too long, and people who don't like action movies will like it because it's got enough boring parts interspersed with the excellent fights to make it seem like Quality Filmmaking. I say less talk, more rock, but this movie will probably have tons of awards by the time you read this, so what the hell do I know, except a boring movie when I see one.

Anyway, the next day is Christmas Eve, and I go and stay with Kirsten in her room for about two and a half hours, which is probably the longest visit we've had yet, and we actually enjoy ourselves just sitting there and watching football, even though Kirsten is a little depressed because her counts are not where she would like them to be, especially if she's going to be on track to go home in three days. When her granulocytes (whatever the hell those are) get to 500 (what is the unit of measure here? I have no idea. Is that 500 total? 500 per milliliter, per liter, per square inch?), she can have the door to her room open. She sort of thought she'd be there by now, but she's only at 350.

Which is just as well, as it turns out, because this time I'm really sure somebody is dying right across the hall. The hall is chock-full of grieving relatives as I am trying to microwave something for Kirsten to eat, and I have to shove past about ten crying people three different times, and when I see a doctor in sweats come in and start hugging people, I know for sure. I look at all these red-eyed people and feel relatively lucky by comparison. I am having a pretty decent afternoon, running around microwaving stuff, sipping Diet Coke through a straw tucked under my mask while watching the Patriots at least give Miami a game, which is more than they've been able to do most of the season, and I look at these people and feel guilty for my cheerful bustling.

And then, right before I am leaving, I remember that it's Christmas Eve, and these people will now always remember standing in this hospital hallway crying while some annoying short bald guy says excuse me every two minutes while someone they love dies. This is their brand-new freshly minted Christmas memory. Merry motherfuckin Christmas.

I head down to Kirsten's folks' house, where Rowen is glad to see me, and after she goes to bed I stay up reading the chess book my friend Eric sent me for Christmas, sadly realizing that I really will never be any good at chess, but enjoying reading about it nonetheless. I have been playing chess for a little over a year now, and while I still suck terribly, I find I can usually beat my students, who, in typical teenage fashion, are way too aggressive and bring the queen out on like the second move, while the tired old man bides his time and usually wins. Except when playing other tired old men with even a little bit of skill, in which case I get shellacked, usually in an embarrassing fashion.

Christmas morning with Kirsten's folks arrives, and the best part of it is the stockings, because they have stuff like pens and dried porcini mushrooms and small kitchen implements in them, and I always enjoy and get use out of the stocking stuff. Rowen gets a ton of gifts but is a distant second to Kirsten's brother's wife, who I guess is my sister-in-law, but I sometimes wish I spoke Chinese or some other language that reflected the importance of kinship and would therefore have a different word for Kirsten's sister and Kirsten's brother's wife, but anyway, Keri gets a boatload of stuff from her parents, who are not here but have mailed a ton of presents from Virginia. And this is like an ad for the voluntary simplicity movement, because she literally has so many gifts piled on the table in front of her that none of us can see her, and okay, she's a small woman, but still. Each present does not seem to bring her increased joy, but rather increased annoyance. She gets cranky after about the third one.

I have been cranky since before we started opening presents, because this whole thing just feels wrong. I had convinced myself that I didn't care, that this Christmas was just going to pass, was just going to be another day, you know, no big deal, but as I sit here on Christmas morning I feel terrible. Where is my wife? Why am I here with her family without her? I have terrible flash-forwards to future joyless Christmases without Kirsten, and all those stupid pop songs I complained about were right—I don't give a shit about presents or anything else—all I want is my wife back, and everything else can go to hell.

I don't mean to slight Kirsten's parents here, because they do their best to make this festive, and we have an enjoyable, relaxed time. They get me a cookbook, and Kirsten's brother gives me a video game I wanted. (Yes, I am now deep enough into this video game thing to have games I want. I have also broken my no-shooting rule before I broke my no-playing-while-Rowen's-awake rule, because my friend Jessie gave me this awesome game where you drive around and try to blow up other cars and your surroundings, and one of the characters in the game has a special secret weapon of a deadly subwoofer that shakes the ground, which incidentally seems to have a real-world counterpart that is in wide circulation in my neighborhood.) But all the same, this sucks.

I call Kirsten, and she is in tears for only the second time since this whole thing started, and I'm crying too (I've lost count), and merry motherfuckin Christmas, ho-ho-ho, this holiday bites. Fortunately there is some kind of conspiracy among the nurses on Kirsten's floor to break the rules and allow Rowen to visit. There is a big sign on the door that says no children under six are allowed, and they had initially told us that they only break that rule when a parent is dying on the floor, but I guess the Christmas spirit has taken over, so Rowen and I head up to the hospital and, under the supervision of Kirsten's primary nurse, who of course I have a crush on (not in a cheesy, naughty-nurse *Playboy* magazine type of way, but, you know, she is kind of attractive and she takes good care of all of us and laughs at Kirsten's jokes, so what's not to like?), we wash up, get Rowen some spiffy Smurfette gloves, and into the bubble we go. Kirsten is sitting up in bed, pale, bald, and smiling. "Hi sweetie!" she says when Rowen comes in. She is really too sick to get out of bed and greet us, and so I expect Rowen to shout "Mommy!" and go running into her arms, but I guess this is weird and scary for her, so she sort of turns into my leg and clings to me. Three weeks ago Rowen used to cry if I picked her up from preschool without Kirsten. Now she totally clings to me and basically won't get off my lap, because I am the new number one.

Eventually Rowen agrees to sit up on Kirsten's bed if she can be on my lap, so the two of us sit there and Kirsten closes her eyes, hugs us both, and says, "Mmmmm, it's so good to see you." I am convinced I am going to start bawling, reunion scenes always get me more than anything, every Christmas I start sobbing when Jimmy Stewart runs into the house, tears in his eyes, yelling, "Zuzu! Kids!" but strangely enough I am able to hold it in during the saddest, happiest reunion I will probably ever see in real life.

After five minutes we all relax a little, and despite the masks and the gloves and the adjustable bed and Kirsten's shiny bald head, we all feel more normal than we have in weeks. The three of us are finally together, and this holiday finally feels like it makes some sense. I get the feeling that if the nurses ran things rather than the doctors, the health care system would be a whole lot less fucked up.

Merry Christmas.

Hooray for a New Day

When Nan was here, she told us that she used to always get her sons up by opening their shades and saying, "Hooray for a new day!" I think I mocked her mercilessly for being a corn dog at the time, but today I sort of feel like shouting hooray for a new day myself.

Rowen and I go out to the movies, which is the perfect thing to do on this freezing cold day because there is a tunnel from the subway station into the mall where the movie theater is, so once we get on the train at our stop, we don't have to go outside again until we come home. We go see *The Emperor's New Groove,* which I like a surprising amount, especially because it lacks most of the stuff that makes Disney movies insufferable, like villains that are too scary and scenes that are too disturbing (when I saw *Tarzan,* kids were screaming as the hunter shot at Tarzan's family), terrible music (I know, I know, "Under the Sea," but I refer you again to *Tarzan,* and its pseudo-jungle Phil Collins songs and to most of the songs in most of the movies), formulaic, stupid talking animal sidekicks (well, the main character in this one gets turned into a llama, but it wasn't the usual wisecracking crab, dragon, meerkat, or whatever), and gratuitous violence (I always wondered how electroshock to the testicles gets an R rating for *The Lords of Discipline,* but merits a G for *101 Dalmatians*). All of which is a rather negative way of saying that I really like this movie and we have a great time and eat way too much popcorn because I am seduced by the "For 25 cents more I can give you the garbage bag instead of the dime bag" routine at the concession stand. I look in the paper the next day and see that this movie has made about ten bucks, so I guess my taste in Disney movies just doesn't match up with most of America's, and which also means that we can probably look forward to more wisecracking ferrets and bad lite-rock soundtracks in future movies.

I go to the hospital, peek my head in the open door, and see the room is empty, and I turn my head and there is Kirsten, pole-free, she has forsaken Baxter and come back to me, and she is just walking down the hallway. "I gotta be seen walking so they'll let me out of here tomorrow," she says. "I also have to keep drinking." She polishes off a Diet Coke and writes it down in her drinking log. She needs to get to two liters today in order to get out tomorrow. I am stunned. Yesterday was one of the worst days yet, we were both crying, she could barely get out of bed, I felt like Ebenezer freaking Scrooge about Christmas, and now she is up smiling and walking around.

I am sure that the docs here at Major Research Hospital would pooh-pooh this idea as unscientific, but I sure as hell think having Rowen in here yesterday had a lot to do with this. Maybe I'm a corn dog too, but this is the most dramatic change I have seen in Kirsten yet—everything so far has been incremental, both on the downside and on the upside, and now all of a sudden there is this quantum leap, and it just doesn't seem coincidental to me that it came after Kirsten finally got to see her daughter after almost three weeks. Like I said, I am sure the docs would mock me—well, no, what they actually would do is try desperately to put this "I'm taking you seriously" face on, but be unable to disguise the "Yeah, whatever, you fucking freak" face trying to break through and say something like, "Yes, well, if it helps you to think that, that's great," or something like that.

I come out of the hospital feeling elated, and after I pick up some stuff at the grocery store and send Kirsten's parents on their way, Rowen and I play her new go fish game—she cheats shamelessly—and put on her favorite CD (R.E.M.'s *Monster*—it is the only thing she ever wants to hear, and I am getting a little tired of it, but it's a tribute to "What's the Frequency, Kenneth?" that I can still stand to hear it after about a month in heavy Rowen rotation, and I count my blessings that it's not, you know, *Barney Sings Calypso* or something horrible like that) and dance around the living room.

Later some guys from church come over to do some clean-ing, and I must digress here and say that these are the only men who have volunteered for this duty, and they happen to be a gay couple, and I don't know what to make of that. With the notable exception of the minister and Emerson the prayer warrior, none of the straight men in the congregation have helped out visibly with any of this stuff, though to be fair a lot of them have proba-bly been home watching kids and stuff while the women were here, but I know if the roles were reversed I might give some-body a ride or cook them a dinner, but I damn sure wouldn't go clean their bathroom, so there you go.

So Robert and Tim are here cleaning and I like having them in the house because they are really kind people who give off good vibes. Rowen is helping me cook some spring rolls while I sip some kick-ass stout. I am pleasantly, mildly buzzed, and I have one of these moments of perfect happiness. I am full of gratitude for the nice people cleaning our house and for Kirsten's turnaround, I am full of love for Rowen and proud and happy that she seems interested in sharing my hobby (as she inexpertly rolls a spring roll, she says, "I wanna help you cook *every* night," and my heart just sings). For several minutes, I am just completely content, and I realize that I am incredibly lucky, sick spouse or no, because I think these moments are just so rare for so many people, and here I am having one right now, and it feels wonderful. Hooray for a new day.

Trickster God

Thinking about God, I can see the appeal of a lot of those old, dead religions that are now, because there are no adherents around to get mad, called "mythology," because they tend to include wacky trickster gods. Well, it's tough to pick out the tricksters in Greek mythology, since they all pretty much are jealous, murderous, lustful, and deceitful, and humans quite frequently come out on the wrong end of those traits. (Zeus the serial rapist literally originates the "golden shower"! It's true! Go check your Edith Hamilton!) These old religions include as part and parcel of the whole thing the idea that the gods are fucking with you just because they can.

Here is more theology that seems to fit the data of my life, especially recently. For example: Christmas. Outside of marveling at the genius of Phil Spector, I tried really hard not to get into the spirit. I even blew off church, which I think I have done maybe two other times that I can remember in my whole life, because even as a kid we used to go to mass with relatives on Christmas Eve, but this year I just couldn't be bothered. I just didn't want to go without Kirsten, I didn't want it to feel like Christmas, but, like the Grinch, I found that I couldn't stop Christmas from coming—it came just the same. Church or no, I felt this horrible void on Christmas.

Then, the day after Christmas Day, the lowest day yet, Kirsten is prowling the halls, practically bouncing off the walls ready to go home. And I am happy, and grateful, but my first reaction is like, "Are you fucking with me?"

Then I have my moment of absolute happiness, but then I wake up in the middle of the night and puke up my spring rolls in my freshly cleaned and disinfected toilet. Okay, I did have another stout, and they were pretty high-octane, but still, we're talking about two beers. And about eight really inexpertly fried spring rolls that were just dripping with peanut oil (I am very vain and usually annoyingly immodest about my cooking ability, like when people at work see me heating up leftovers and say, "That smells great," I am an incredible wiener and say something like "It is great. I made it") because I can't deep-fry anything for shit, so after the best day and night I have had in weeks, possibly months, there I am hunched over the toilet in the middle of the night puking up acidy, oily goo.

What am I to make of all this? We have a wonderful, healthy kid, and this causes our neighbor to get in touch with the asshole within. We get a great deal on a new house and then find that Kirsten has cancer. Kirsten tolerates the chemo very well, and then we find out it doesn't work. I am grateful that it's not all bad, because God knows there are plenty of people in real life as well as in Dennis Lehane novels who live lives of unrelenting misery—I am still incredibly grateful for the night with the spring rolls. The memory of that moment is not tainted or ruined by the fact that I puked six hours later. I feel like that's good, like that must mean I'm making progress, but still . . . I feel like someone's fucking with me.

And I am worried, because now, three days later, Kirsten is home from the hospital, tired, but herself. It is magical to have her in the house again, things feel right, I feel whole, Rowen is happy (I slipped down to number two parent in a hurry, but I am not taking it personally), and I can't shake the feeling that right now while I'm standing up, some asshole is putting a tack on my chair.

Vacation

Kirsten returning home is like a second honeymoon or something: we spend the first two or three days just saying, "I'm glad you're home," or, in her case, "It's good to be home," and every night that I crawl into bed and she is there pressing her freezing cold feet against me I am just so thankful to have her here.

After two days, she has to go to the hospital for a checkup, and they tell her she's dangerously dehydrated and keep her there all day pumping fluids into her veins. They tell her she has to be much better about drinking, so the rest of the vacation she is constantly drinking something, and when she's not, I am going, "Can I get you something? Tea? Soda? Water?" and she writes it all down in her drinking log, until her mom tidies up her drinking log by mistake one day (because it's scrawled on the back of an envelope—it's an easy mistake to make), so Kirsten takes to wearing this stitch counter that she has for knitting projects, using it to total up her daily fluid intake.

Saturday we are expecting a big snowstorm—six to twelve inches. I think about getting a snowblower, but by the time I get my lazy ass over to Home Depot, they are all sold out, so I figure well, it's vacation, I've got time to shovel, no big deal, so I buy fifty pounds of salt and fifty pounds of sand and one of those crooked-handled back-saver shovels and figure I'll make do the old-fashioned way.

I am once again right across the giant, treacherous, freezing-cold parking lot from Toys "R" Us, so I once again go and ogle the game selection, even though I haven't really gotten good at the ones I have yet, not to mention the fact that Toys "R" Us after Christmas looks kind of like this bare-shelved Soviet-era toy store. But I realize that it's more about owning them than wanting to play them. I want to own lots of them. And then what? I won't die, or Kirsten won't die, or somehow sitting on our broke asses amidst a pile of game cases, we'll be secure. I end up not buying any.

I would like to add that video games sure have changed since my day (yes, I know, stupid old-man comment). What I remember about video games was that you could usually get past the first level, or screen, or opponent, or whatever with very little skill, and that with a lot of time and/or quarters invested, you could get good enough to move on. But games today are incredibly hard to even start. The game that Kirsten's brother gave me has this little test you have to pass in order to continue the game. I have been trying for three days, and I'm almost there, but I still haven't gotten into the real game because I keep failing the test of driving skills. I guess these games are designed with dorks like I used to be in mind, rather than with dorks like I currently am in mind. I mean, yeah, if you're sixteen, what the hell else are you going to do except sit in front of your TV for fifteen hours trying to figure out a game, and anyway it costs you the equivalent of maybe four or five hours of folding sweaters at the Gap or whatever, so you're going to be pissed off if it can't hold your interest for a long long time. Whereas if you're thirty-two and get to play an hour every other day, what you really want is something you can be kinda good at without really trying, and that you can get steadily better at. Like Defender, or Pac-Man, or something. Sigh. Time has moved on and left me in the dust clutching my joystick.

But I was talking about the snowstorm. So the thing is that one of Rowen's classmates has a birthday party scheduled for that day. I call in the morning hoping that it's been canceled, but it hasn't, and it's half an hour away at a location of small children's activity centers, so I am annoyed going over there, and I am hoping that it's going to start snowing early in the morning so we can beg off, but of course what happens is that the first flakes start to fall as we pull into the parking lot.

There is something about parties that just brings out the misanthrope in me these days. I see all these other parents, and I just can't stand them. I guess because there is this gulf between us. We are not good friends (not because I hate them or anything, but, you know, I have never seen one of them outside school and birthday parties, so I don't really know them very well), so I don't feel comfortable talking about what's really happening with us right now, and yet I am also completely unable to make pleasant conversation. I have always been terrible at this anyway, but my meager abilities at making small talk have completely disappeared. So I just kind of sit and sulk, and Rowen clings to me, which I think is sort of strange because the kids at this party are the same kids she spends all day playing with. I look at her and remember being shy as a kid, and how I was just so afraid of joining in with groups of other kids (looking at my behavior with adults, I guess not too much has changed), and I see her doing this, and it just kind of makes me sad, because I think I missed out on a lot of fun as a kid because I was afraid.

And yet, looking at what's happening here, I sort of have to applaud Rowen's discernment. We are at this Children's Activity Center™, and there is this woman running the show, and I have to say that whoever put this "curriculum" together knew a lot about little kids, because this woman sings a song, leads some kind of activity, and then tells the kids they can run around on the play equipment for a few minutes. All of which is cool, but this woman is just so obviously not into it, even though she sings well (making sure to mention the corporate name in just about every song—e.g., "We're spreading out the parachute, parachute, parachute, we're spreading out the parachute, here at

Children's Activity Center™," which I find kind of creepy). Still, most of the kids have a great time and get to do some kind of rambunctious play on a shitty day.

We leave, and the drive home is not too bad, because the snow is really slushy, so it's not too slippery, and as we get home, the snow turns into rain. Which is pretty close to a quote from a Dan Fogelberg song, if I remember correctly, and as much as I think he's a cheese merchant, I have to give him credit that that's a pretty good line for summing up something magical turning into something depressing. (How about that "Leader of the Band" song, though—what's up with "his blood runs through my instrument"? Eeewww!)

And I get cranky and surly that this storm that I was dreading driving through has fizzled into a crappy rainstorm, because I love snow. I think this pretty well typifies my attitude these days: I am pissed about having to drive through a storm, then pissed when the storm turns out to be not as hazardous as I feared. As much as I have questioned God through this whole thing, on this day I can just imagine her (I sort of like to think of God as female, 'cause I think, well, if God were female [and yes, I think it's kind of puerile to assign God a gender, but what the hell, so is quoting Dan Fogelberg], she would pretty much have to be a total babe)—ahem, I can just imagine God looking down at me going, "Jesus! What the hell do you want? There's just no pleasing you, is there?"

Nope.

Sick of It

While it is of course wonderful to have Kirsten home and it is lucky that she is released during a time when I am off from work, I find that the hustle and bustle of the time when she was in the hospital was in some way easier.

I mean, yeah, I complained a lot, but when you are just go-go-going all the time, you don't have much time to stop and think. Whereas when you are not go-go-going very much at all, there is little else to do but think. I should say at the outset here that I don't do vacations well. I never have. That is to say, if I go away, I can do a vacation just fine—I am happy to hang out, take naps, and basically do nothing at all for days at a time. But when I am at home, I start to get squirrelly after a few days. It's a kind of funny contradiction, because on the one hand, I consider myself to be fundamentally a pretty lazy person, but on the other hand, I have to work or I go insane.

So I always start getting bored and depressed after about a week of time off at home, and this is no exception. In fact, it's much worse than usual, because now I am thinking about our situation all the time. Since I have nothing else to define myself by, I become Brendan Halpin, Spouse of a Cancer Patient. And since I don't have to run anywhere or do anything, I get to contemplate all the stuff I wasn't thinking about before. When she was in the hospital, I just took it as a given that this treatment would work. But what if it doesn't? And even under the best of circumstances, we're not really talking about a cure here. We're talking about keeping it at bay for a period of time.

Now that Kirsten is out of the hospital, it makes contemplating the next round that much harder, because we know what it's going to be like, but also, having just come out of something so difficult, I am now sick to fucking death of this whole thing. I have found this before—you know, the job, or the apartment, or whatever that you have had for years suddenly becomes intolerable after you know you are going to leave. At least that's the way it's always been for me—I never got all misty-eyed thinking of the colleagues I'd never see again, or thinking of the street I'd rarely walk down again. My reaction has always been, "I can't wait to get away from this horrible place and these horrible people," and while it would seem logical that little annoyances would bug you less in these circumstances, they get magnified, so you're just like, "I can't fucking wait to get out of this fucking place!"

Well, I can't fucking wait to get out of this fucking place. I am sick of being sad, I'm sick of worrying, I'm sick of having people look meaningfully into my eyes and say, "So how *is* Kirsten?" I'm sick of having to rely on people's kindness to keep my house clean, I'm sick of thinking about it, I'm sick to fucking death of living in the shadow of cancer and of having that be what defines me and Kirsten and Rowen to everybody else, and to ourselves. There they go, that brave family, how do they keep their sense of humor through all this, isn't it sweet how he shaved his head, my but that kid seems to be doing well, considering, I just don't know how they do it, I know I would fall apart if it was me, thank God it's not me. I just want to be a normal person again.

And the thing is, I can't. I can't ever. I realize that I have been fooling myself. I have been thinking that once the second round of treatment is over, that that's when we get our normal lives back. But the sad fact is that we never ever get our lives back like we had them before. There will always be appointments, and drugs, and possibly surgeries, and maybe new drugs, and encouraging test results and discouraging test results, and unless I fall over dead in three years like my dad, I will probably, in ten years, or fifteen, or twenty, have to put Kirsten in the ground, or else burn her up and try to figure out how to live then. And I don't even know how to live now.

I feel like I've been on hold for three months (Please continue to hold. Your life is important to us), and my thought has been, well, as soon as we get our lives back, I can stop eating like a hog, as soon as things are back to normal I will stay on top of my planning and correcting, as soon as this is over I will take a deep breath and get back to living like a normal person again. But I won't. This disease has stolen that life from me, and from Kirsten, and worst of all from Rowen, and we can't wait for later to figure out how to put a life together. We have to do it now. But I don't know how.

Fuckin' Up

On January 2, Kirsten and I go to the grocery store. We will later be chastised for this by Dr. J and two nurses, who are incredulous that we didn't understand when they gave us this discharge booklet that said, "Try to avoid crowds," that that meant Kirsten was basically supposed to be under house arrest. I guess they have done this so much that they think it's obvious, and they forget that this is our first time through this. Bad communication.

Anyway, speaking of bad communication, we are in the grocery store, and as we are stuffing oranges into a produce bag, Kirsten says, "So how exactly did the plan for this week get changed?"

"Uhhhhhhh. Yeah . . ." Shit. I am busted. We had agreed that I would take the whole week after vacation off to take care of her. And then, before vacation, I established that Tuesday was a professional development day which I could blow off with no problem, and Wednesday I got a former colleague to come in and give an introduction to the *Odyssey* lecture, and if anything at all was going to happen for the rest of the week, I was going to have to spend some serious time planning and writing up sub plans, which I couldn't really do before vacation because I was running around too much, and then Kirsten came home and it just sort of got away from me, so what I did was just sort of change the default plan from taking all four days off to taking two days off. I will say in my defense that if Kirsten had really been bedridden and everything, I certainly would have stayed home.

Okay, now for the ugly part. Well, the first part of the ugly part. The really ugly part, the ugliest part of all, is that I can't stand to take any time off of work. There were the practical considerations of what was planned for the classes to do, but the bottom line is that I love to work and I need to work to keep me sane, and it is my favorite thing right now. I felt guilty about saying that in our planning conversations. How can you possibly say to your sick spouse that you want to spend as little time as possible at home with her because you love to work so much? I, for one, am way too much of a coward to say that, and also it would have entailed me revealing what an asshole I am, so I just revealed what an asshole I am with my actions instead, by changing the plan without talking to Kirsten about it.

And now she is calling me on it in the supermarket. And so, up and down the aisles we have the conversation, and I reveal what I just said about how I didn't know how to assert how important work was to me, and she says, next to the juice boxes, "It just makes me sad that after twelve years we are still having this bad communication."

As we round the corner to the cereal aisle, she says, "I mean . . . I've tried to get other people to do stuff whenever I could. My mom came up, your mom came up, Nan came up. It just doesn't seem like you've done that much."

I am dumbstruck. She's wrong. That is so terribly unfair. She's right. I don't say anything until we get to the canned tomatoes, because I don't know whether to agree and apologize or fight back. "What?" she says. "What are you thinking?"

"I guess . . . I guess I really don't think that's fair," I manage. "I've done a lot." She backs off, and we check out, and then head to the car, where she starts to cry. Now, Kirsten is not the kind of person who cries a lot. Whereas I cry all the time, when Kirsten cries it is an event. I can probably remember each time she has cried since I've known her.

So now tears are falling and I have caused them. "It's not easy for me to ask for help," she says, and she cries and cries and I feel like the total shit that I am. I start apologizing profusely, and she accepts, and I continue apologizing until my apologizing becomes incredibly annoying, and she says, "I understand. You can stop apologizing. It's done now. I'll be fine. I just need to be sad for a while." This is just a knife in my heart. It's worse than the tears. I offer to take those days off, but the truth is she doesn't really need me around to help, she just needs me to have wanted to, and I couldn't do that, and there is nothing I can do to go back and make this right.

After all I have thought and heard about guys who have affairs during this time, I have become them. Not because I have slept with anyone else, but because I betrayed my wife while she was sick. Yeah, I've done a lot of stuff, but when she asked me to give up the thing that means the most to me, when she, the love of my life, my best friend, asked me to pick her over work, I didn't do it. I have willingly done all kinds of stuff, but she is right in a sense that I haven't done much, because everything else I have done hasn't really involved making sacrifices for her.

I feel like a total dick. I guess that's because I am a total dick.

I find myself trying to think and rationalize all day, trying to think of a way I can not be the guy who did something shitty and made his wife—his wife who's sick with cancer, his wife who never cries—cry, but I can't.

I call Danny, and he listens and says, yeah, I fucked up, but, you know, people fuck up, and I should really make some kind of gesture that says I fucked up and please forgive me, and that even though a flower delivery or something seems cheesy, especially to smart, savvy women like our wives, it tends to work anyway. "Great," I say, "except we're not allowed to have flowers or chocolate in the house." True. It's part of Kirsten's low-immunity regime. The chocolate part is killing her.

So I can't do anything except be contrite, and she is not one of these people who hold a grudge and mope around for days, so she seems to forgive me pretty quickly. But then, of course, it will be a hell of a long time before I can forgive myself.

Back to School

I go back to school one day after the students do, and it is wonderful. I have to get there a little bit later than I'm used to, because Kirsten still needs to sleep a lot and is not really ready to take over the parenting duties at 7:00 A.M., so I take Rowen to preschool an hour and a half earlier than she's used to going. She is a pretty good sport about it, considering. She hates change, and while it's true that, yes, she does spend the entire walk on the first day moaning, "I'm tiiiiiired . . . I'm tiiiiiired . . . ," and she does spend most of the second day moaning, "I'm colllllllllld . . . I'm colllllllllld" (Superdad forgot her hat and mittens when it was like 20 degrees outside), she does not get hysterical or throw tantrums, and it seems to be okay. Also, groaning and all, I look forward to any time the two of us get to have together.

So I drop her off, hop on the subway, and head to school. One of the first things I do is find the girl I was shitty to about the bus pass on the day before vacation and apologize. She has no memory at all of what I am talking about and looks at me like I am vaguely insane for bringing it up. I find this happens the majority of times when I am kicking myself for saying something unkind to a kid—I end up apologizing, and they don't even remember what I am talking about. I have two theories on this: one is that they are just so used to teachers being assholes to them that they kind of don't notice, and the other is that I am a little too hard on myself. Probably both things are true.

Classes go surprisingly well, given the fact that I haven't had time or energy to plan anything, and I actually do find time to start wading through the mountain of papers I have to correct that I didn't do before vacation, and I can start thinking and worrying about other things besides cancer, like my advisees and their big and small crises, and like how I am living a live-action version of *Animal Farm* with humans.

Maybe I should explain. As I said, I teach in a charter school, and our founders, we'll call them Snowball and Napoleon, were teachers in a large urban public school and were appalled by the stupidity and/or evil of the institution they worked for and were sure that, as teachers, they could do better. So they started their own school.

Which is a hell of a gutsy move and which I admire them for. I think their instinct that teachers know what they are doing is pretty sound (though I can certainly think of a whole raft of exceptions from places I have worked), and without them the school would not exist, and teaching in this school is pretty much my dream job, so I am grateful to them.

Except now neither Snowball nor Napoleon is teaching anymore, but they are still on the board, and the board is now telling us that we need to create a position for someone primarily concerned with grants and PR, and that the teachers and principal should report to that person. In other words, they want to give us a superintendent and totally duplicate the fucked-up structure of the fucked-up schools that this school was supposed to be a counterexample to. Four legs good, two legs better.

I get angry about what appears to be a really bad move from any number of perspectives, but, and I know this is not true of my colleagues, for me it is a fun kind of angry. Because the bottom line is that whether we turn into just another fucked-up school or not matters a whole hell of a lot less to me than Kirsten living or dying. So this fight to me is like the video games I've been playing. Sure I want to kill the guy in the hoopty pickup who attacks my lethal subwoofer-equipped car with a swarm of mutant bees, but when it's game over I am not really that disturbed. (Except, you know, at myself for engaging in this simulated violence that goes against pretty much everything I believe and also for getting so into it. Sometimes Kirsten wanders in while I'm playing and asks what's going on, and I have to sheepishly explain that I am trying to stop a guy with a specially modified deadly disco ball from destroying Las Vegas by rippling the ground below him with deadly bass.) Fighting about this proposed change in the school feels like the same thing. It's fun while it lasts, but I am not really losing any sleep over it. I have taught in fucked-up schools before, and as long as I can work with kids I will find a way to be happy.

Also, I really like my colleagues. One day, sort of out of the blue, this woman that I know only slightly comes into my classroom while I am sitting there shooting the shit with somebody, and tells me that she had a girlfriend who had cancer—well, she is circumspect about saying "girlfriend," she uses those careful phrases like "I was with someone" and "this person" (which I guess gay people probably get used to saying for protection, which is a damn sad statement about us breeders) had cancer— and she says all she as the cancer patient's partner could stand to do was work. And, she says, her co-workers, friends, and family didn't understand, they all thought she should be at home all the time, but she just had to work or she would go insane. And I explain that I feel the same way, and she tells me that she knows exactly how I feel, and that she understands.

She doesn't give me any platitudes or empty reassurances or advice or even offers to talk when I need to that I would have to awkwardly thank her for and then feel vaguely guilty for not following up on. She just says that she understands. This is just such a tremendous gift. I am genuinely touched, and I thank her, but I am not sure it was profuse enough, because she has done something wonderful. She has done God's work.

I think this is why the idea of Jesus having been God is so important to so many Christians (though, as I've said, not especially to me)—because it implies that God was human and so fully understands what we are going through. And I have to admit that that's a nice idea, but then if you say, well, if Jesus was human, he must have had uncontrollable boners when he was thirteen, you get people wanting to burn you at the stake, so maybe I understand their belief system a little less than I think I do.

I don't know whether Jesus was God, or God was Jesus, or whether either of them had uncontrollable boners when they were thirteen (though every human male I know did), but I do know that for me, today, God's face is the face of a gray-haired lesbian who tells me she understands me.

The Heroic Trio

Friday night I decide to do something wackier and rowdier than I have done in years: I go to a midnight movie. Now I know that this probably doesn't sound like much of a bender, but keep in mind that I have been a high school teacher for eight years and have never started work later than 7:30 A.M., and I have been a parent for four years, and can't remember ever sleeping past 7:30 A.M. even on a weekend in all that time, so doing anything that's going to get me home at 2:00 A.M. is just totally out of character and seems incredibly rowdy, which I guess tells you how deeply deeply lame I am.

I almost don't make it. The first week of school after a vacation is always exhausting, and this is the same week in which I pulled my Judas routine (though I like to think of it as a milder betrayal, so let's say my Saint Peter routine), so I am still kind of emotionally worn out, and at about 9:00 P.M. Kirsten crawls into bed and I go to tuck her in and say I'll just lie down for a few minutes, and she tells me that I have to stay up or I'll feel like absolute shit, so I get up and power through the fatigue and grogginess.

I head over to the theater. I should say that I have come here not to see just any movie. This is *The Heroic Trio,* which I have rented many times but never seen on a big screen. It is an action movie from Hong Kong about three beautiful superheroes who have to fight first each other and then an androgynous demon who lives below the city and who is kidnapping babies looking for the next Chinese emperor. And who shoots poison needles from his or possibly her fingers. It features some really spectacular fights, an evil guy who gets his finger cut off and then eats it, some cool decapitations, and one scene where a spinning, flying motorcycle is used as a weapon. Did I mention that the heroines are all fantastic babes? Plus it has tragedy, comedy, lots of fighting on wires, and you never have to wait more than five minutes to see some really spectacular asskicking, and also the ending pretty much makes sense, all of which is in marked contrast to a certain other martial arts movie that since I wrote about it has been nominated for three Golden Globe awards, which I know are basically pieces of crap, remember Pia Zadora won one, but still, I was right about the awards thing.

Anyway, this movie looks really cool—a lot of it is shot through blue filters, and it has some pretty good sets, so I decide that seeing it on the big screen will be worth it. But when I get to the theater, I am kind of aghast at the crowd. First of all, I am a solid five years older than the next oldest person here, and ten years older than most of the people here. I feel like I'm about seventy-five. This comes only days after I hit another old-man milestone when I switched the radio button that for years belonged to the "alternative" station to the classic rock station. Classic rock is not exactly my favorite format, and as a youth I wore my allegiance to "alternative" music as this badge of protest against dinosaur rock hegemony, but I have reached an age where I would much rather hear "Sympathy for the Devil" than, for example, Limp Bizkit or Rage Against the Machine screaming at me or Eminem bitching about how hard it is to be famous.

Secondly, these people at the theater are like caricatures of college-studenty hipsters. When I walk up to the box office I literally have to wade through a cloud of clove cigarette smoke. I mean, clove cigarettes. Please.

But hey, I was twenty-one once, and God knows I was ridiculous (though, I would say in contrast to most of these people, not ridiculously tattooed or pierced), so I should just shut up. I meet my friend Lisa from work (who's a lesbian, so it's not like I'm having some kind of date while Kirsten sleeps, okay?). She also likes watching beautiful women kick the shit out of people, though I think she comes at it from more of a female empowerment angle than my own prurient angle. This despite the fact that she's a Quaker and therefore morally opposed to all asskicking. Well, everybody's complicated.

Anyway, they tell us that there will be a short performance before the movie, and I am very nervous about this because the woman who sells me my ticket says, "It's some kind of mime thing," but it ends up being a very funny excerpt from this guy's one-man show in which he plays this mime teacher who's been forced to teach a combination mime–rap–tae kwon do class. The movie totally kicks my ass, even though they have found an incredibly shitty print that must have been sitting in the basement of some Malaysian theater for the last five years. In addition to the action, there is a very sad scene where one of the babies dies, and another kind of moving scene where the one woman's boyfriend dies, and even though, yes, it's about decapitation and women who turn invisible, run across power lines, or ride a 55-gallon drum with an explosive charge in the back into a hostage situation, two of the three have worked for the androgynous demon before turning good, so it is also really about redemption. But not so much that you sit there going, "Okay, okay, enough about redemption, kick somebody's ass already." And Michelle Yeoh is really breathtaking in this movie, except in the admittedly laughable part where the skeleton of the androgynous demon has wrapped itself around her and made her fight her friends against her will.

I get home at 2:00 A.M., and I feel like complete shit the next day, but I am really glad I went.

Sunday Morning Coming Down

By Sunday morning I have almost recovered from my Friday night movie extravaganza. Rowen and I go to church but Kirsten has to stay home—apparently her T cells, which are the virus fighters, won't be back to normal strength for a year, so it is basically a bad idea for her to go inside where there will be lots of people during flu season. This is why Dr. J and the nurses yelled at us about going grocery shopping.

It is the first Sunday of the new year, and in our church at the beginning of each new year we light candles and share hopes and concerns for the new year. First we have a little mini-sermon. The minister manages to slip a fun factoid into his sermon, which is the reason why the symbol of Unitarian Universalism is a flaming chalice. We have always had this thing in our order of service that said the flaming chalice "commemorates the spirit of reformer Jan Hus" or some such thing, but this guy says that what Jan Hus did was to share the communion chalice around the congregation, which was a big no-no at the time he did it, 450 years ago or whenever, so they burned him at the stake. Now anybody who's giving communion regularly shares out the chalice. Wonder if they've ever officially retracted the order to fry his ass. Anyway, we don't get this kind of blood-and-guts, martyr-for-the-faith stuff much in a Unitarian church, so I dig it.

When it's time for those who feel so moved to light candles, I make my way to the front, because I feel that it's really important to thank people, I mean the members of this church are still cleaning our bathroom all the time—they've stepped it up to nightly now, not to mention doing a deep clean on Saturdays—and it helps us a lot and makes us feel loved, so I have been calmly rehearsing this thing I want to say. And then I get to the mike and I can't say it. I start to cry. The congregation nicely waits while I collect myself. Here is what I eventually say: "My hope for the new year is that my wife, Kirsten, can be healed this year, and that other people who are suffering can feel the same love and support that we have gotten from friends, family, and from this church."

I walk back to my pew and I see several people crying, and some people kind of grab me by the arm or the hand or whatever, and while I meant everything I said, there is the hammy performer side of me that is looking around at these teary faces and going, "Man! I knocked 'em dead! I killed!"

Probably I'll go to hell for that.

After the service, lots of people come up to me and say nice things, and people I barely know tell me that they pray for Kirsten every night, which is pretty spectacular. Many people also thank me for saying what I said, which initially seems kind of odd to me, but I guess my getting up there and saying something real and personal made the service seem more important, or something. I don't know. Being Unitarians, we usually get a lot of "My hope is that the people of Nicaragua . . . etc. etc.," and I like the people of Nicaragua as much as the next guy, but those things usually don't move me much when I hear them the way that personal things do, so maybe that's why people are thanking me.

Kirsten's folks are coming for dinner, so Rowen and I go to

the grocery store to pick up a few extra things. When we get back to the house at about 1:30, her folks are there and Kirsten is in tears.

As I have said, her crying is an event, so I am immediately trying to figure out what's going on, but she won't talk about it. I figure she must have been telling the story of me being a dick and she got upset again, so I keep pestering her to tell me what's up, and she finally says, "We were just having a little heart-to-heart."

Well you could just about knock me over with a feather. Heart-to-hearts are pretty unheard of in Kirsten's family. Indeed, in the twelve years we've been together, this is the first one I can remember even hearing about, except for a bungled facts-of-life talk from her early adolescence that was something like, "You guys are learning about that in school, right?"

So there is weirdness in the air, and Kirsten's parents leave after about an hour, and I say to her, "I thought they were staying for dinner," and she says, "Yeah, well, I guess they decided not to." She then starts to cry again, and she reveals how the talk started out as banter about "Get off my back, mom" kinda stuff, and it eventually worked its way around to her mom saying, more or less, "You never tell me anything, that's why I bug you with annoying questions all the time, and we're doing the best we can and trying to help out, and you're always pushing us away." And she can't really deny any of that, and she feels guilty and horrible, and as a result she becomes thoroughly depressed, getting into this funk that's almost exactly where I was a week ago, just feeling incredibly tired of all this and wanting it to be over. (I guess it says a lot about our respective personal strength that I reached this point before Kirsten, who is actually sick, did.)

I am sad because Kirsten's illness seems to be pulling at the fault lines in both of our relationships with our parents. I tell Kirsten that it's not her fault that she doesn't have the kind of relationship with her parents where she shares her innermost thoughts with them, because she's never had that kind of relationship with them, and it has never really appeared to be a problem before, so if they want something different now, it's kind of too bad.

I am also sad because, as much as this whole thing has demonstrated to me the depths of people's selflessness, it also seems to show that there is a limit, and that most of us, and yes, I certainly include myself here, have a hard time being completely selfless. And so my mom comes here to help out, but there is something she wants, and she gets mad when she doesn't get it, and so I weasel out of it when Kirsten asks me for help, and so Kirsten's folks are making demands on her, and what we should all do is just shut the fuck up and do exactly as much or as little as she wants us to and worry about how we feel about it later. Why can't we do this? I guess we can all talk a pretty good game about putting someone else first, but when it comes down to it, we can't really do it.

Kirsten is lower now than she has been since this whole thing started. I am so worried about her that the next day I secretly call Jen and ask her to arrange for regular visits and phone calls to keep Kirsten's spirits up. And the visits and phone calls come, but Kirsten seems to snap out of this on her own after a day.

I wish I had about half her strength, but what I really wish is that she didn't need so much.

Let's All Go to the Lobby

Kirsten bounces back from her depression quickly, and though she is still not anywhere near a hundred percent, we have a nice little intermission for a few weeks. She is, of course, still bald, but she seems more like herself than she has in a long time—since we are not constantly running to stressful, painful tests and she is not stuck in the hospital, this is the closest we have had to a normal life in months. Dr. J tells her that her tumor markers are now half what they were, which is good news.

For the first time in months, I am able to think about stuff besides Kirsten being sick. Here are some examples:

I actually manage to drag up some outrage about the way the election was stolen, which I didn't really care about much while it was happening, and I marvel at the guy who is supposed to be the attorney general saying nice things about the Confederacy and wonder how the South, which I always think of as the most rah-rah America part of America, just loves its historical anti-American traitors. Go figure.

I listen constantly to the U2 record that my mom left here. She asks me to send it to her and I totally refuse, and, laughing, she asks if I don't at least feel guilty for basically stealing from her, and I say no. I guess it is a strange and somewhat uncharacteristic moral lapse, but I don't feel the least bit guilty.

We have Rowen's fourth birthday party, and it ends up being fun despite the fact that three of her friends cancel on the day of the party because they all have the same puke-causing illness.

She gets a fair amount of Barbie stuff, and I think Barbie is pretty heinous for a number of reasons, but all the girls at school have them, and I guess I don't feel strongly enough about it to forbid them in the house or anything like that. I guess I hope that if we raise Rowen with good ideas of what being a girl is about that she will be able to overcome Barbie's evil counter-messages. Or maybe she will grow up to drive a hot pink Corvette and live in a Malibu dream house, and what the hell, I guess you could do worse.

I have a few dreams about the Troll and his wife in which we sort of reconcile. When I wake up, I think these dreams are very strange, because I don't think I care whether they hate me or not, and I also know that no kind of reconciliation is possible. If you're going to reconcile with someone, that involves both parties sort of giving a little and admitting that they could have done this or that thing differently, but the thing about these people is that whenever we made such overtures in the past, they interpreted it not as an opening for them to also give a little, but rather as confirmation of their view that we were wrong wrong wrong and they were right right right. I think I may be right about the fact that I don't care whether they like me or not, despite my dreams. I think what's hurting me is that I still hate them. I really do. And I know it makes me a shitty person, and my subconscious mind is telling me to let it go already, but how do you do that? How do you forgive someone who isn't sorry? How do you change how you feel about someone you never speak to? I don't know, but I hope I can figure out a way to stop dragging my hate around.

Danny comes to town, and it is great to see him. We go out

a few times, and you can tell these are rowdy outings because I have two drinks, and we sit in bars and do what ridiculous married men do: we look at the attractive young women in the bar and go, "Oooh, I think she's really cute. . . ." "Yeah, she's more your type than mine. That one over there, on the other hand . . ." You get the idea. Pathetic.

I should say, in fairness to Danny, that we spend a lot of time talking about work, politics, and movies, and that we do actually act like adults for most of the time, though we also do act like we're sixteen—well, sort of, I mean we don't actually play Dungeons and Dragons, but you know what I mean.

Our life at home now seems like a bald version of what it used to be. I know that Kirsten's second hospitalization is coming up, but I am totally in denial. I feel like my normal life is coming back. These two weeks are the first time since the diagnosis that I have felt happy in an uncomplicated way. That is to say, they haven't been tinged by worry, or sadness, or pain. Sure, we're both still bald, and Kirsten still has to be careful about being in crowds and stuff (well, actually I am sure Dr. J would have a heart attack if she knew half the stuff Kirsten has been doing, such as dropping Rowen off at preschool with all of those septic, just-got-over-a-puking-virus-that-could-lay-Kirsten-out-for-weeks little kids running around, but they gave her instructions that were basically impossible for any human to follow, which were basically, get out of the house, but don't actually go anywhere where you might come into contact with other humans. This limits your options quite severely in Boston in January), but we are together and we are happy.

As I write this, I know in my mind that Kirsten is going back in the hospital tomorrow, but it still doesn't feel real. I am so desperate for us to have our life back that I think we do already. But we don't, and there are really no guarantees that we will. I miss it so much.

Act 2, Scene 1

I get up on Friday morning, and all my uncomplicated happiness seems like a weird dream. It's like someone has thrown a switch, and I am suddenly grumpy and hassled again. I wake Rowen up, and she complains terribly while moaning and groaning. It takes her forever to get up and moving, so I figure I will drive her to school so I can get to work on time. I look out the window and discover that this will be impossible because somebody is parked in front of our driveway.

I run downstairs to look at the car. I think it must have been stolen and abandoned, because the doors are unlocked, which is very very unusual in this neighborhood where everybody has a poorly calibrated, screeching, whooping alarm that goes off whenever a heavy truck rumbles by, and the windows are open. I figure the car's gun-toting owner will round the corner the minute I try to get inside to move it, so I decline to get inside. Also I am pretty sure I wouldn't be able to get it out of park without the key.

I go in and call parking enforcement, and, miraculously, they show up in about ten minutes. They slap a ticket on the windshield and leave. I guess I have to hand it to them for the lightning-quick response, but, you know, I still can't move my fucking car.

So I am feeling frustrated, and I watch as the minutes tick off the clock, and I am doing all these mental calculations trying to figure out if there is any way I can get to work on time, and as Rowen is getting ready, she says, "Daaa—aad. Don't look at me." This is not any kind of modesty—this is just one of those things that she insists on and gets furious if it's violated. It's because she doesn't want us to see her until she is dressed in her outfit so it will be a surprise. I assure her that I am not looking at her. I am down the hallway and could not see into her room even if I was trying to. She repeats: "Don't look at me!"

"Honey, I am not looking at you, now will you please hurry up and get your snowsuit on, because we have to leave and I'm going to be late for work!" She repeats that I am not to look at her. After about two more minutes of this, I totally lose my mind and start yelling at her that she has to get ready, that I can't possibly stand here arguing about whether I am looking at her for one more second because I am going to be late, and will you zip up that snowsuit NOW!

Well, I admit this is kind of a pain in the ass right now, and I am sure that some of you will read this and cluck at my permissiveness and say how parents being afraid to use the belt is ruining this country, but Rowen is totally not cowed by my anger. It just infuriates her. She screams right back at me. I hope this means that she will be the kind of person who won't take any shit when she gets older. Then, again, taking shit is a talent that will keep you gainfully employed and generally make your life easier, so maybe I shouldn't wish that on her. Still, I always admire people who are not intimidated by authority figures, even though it is a giant pain in the ass when I am the authority figure in question. I am not really rational enough to think this out right now, though, so I scream back at her. At one point I pick her up so as to carry her out the door.

It is 7:30 in the morning, and I am already in a screaming contest with a four-year-old. This is not a good way to begin the day. I go to another room and leave her to put her snowsuit on, and I immediately feel guilty. I did not swear at her or hit her, but I did completely lose it with her, and I feel like a dick. Like she doesn't have enough stress with mommy going into the hospital, dad has to turn into Mr. Hyde too. Ugh.

If you don't have kids, you probably think that I am completely unhinged, but if you do have kids, I guess you have probably been where I am—as much as I try to stay calm and remind myself that she is four and I am thirty-two, sometimes I just dive right into the sandbox and have a tantrum of my own. Anyway, if you have kids I hope you've been where I am now, because it comforts me a lot to think that I'm not the only terrible parent out there, so if you've never lost it with a kid, just keep your mouth shut and let me cling to my pathetic illusion.

I call work and get Sydney to cover my advisory, and I end up getting there only five minutes late, so what was I so mad about? Besides some dickhead stealing a car and ditching it right across my driveway and the fact that, oh yeah, Kirsten has cancer, and here she goes into the hospital again.

I teach my classes and come home early, which means I get

to miss part two of our personality test seminar. Part one told me I was emotional, disorganized, and messy. Like I need a Myers-Briggs assessment to tell me that. I cry at cartoons and my desk is covered in mountains of crap. I may not be completely self-aware, but I did know that much. Oh yeah, and I both hate people and crave their company. Knew that too.

Anyway, I get home and the car is still there. Kirsten called parking enforcement again, and they quickly promised to tow before she could even guilt them about how we need the car to take her to the hospital today. And then they didn't come and tow the car. We examine the situation and decide that she can direct me in such a way that I can pull the car out at an angle (now I am glad that we haven't gotten around to making our disgusting, completely paved yard into a real yard yet) and drive over the noncut part of the curb.

We manage to do it and only break the fence a little bit as we head off to the hospital. It is old-home week there on the bubble unit, as nurses and cleaners smile and say hi to us and seem sort of glad to see us. One of the nurse's aides reveals that they actually *are* glad to see us, because Kirsten doesn't give them any trouble, so they all like her.

A very cute nurse I've never seen before is in charge of checking us in, and she tells us that they haven't cleaned Kirsten's room yet, so we need to go wait in the solarium. This is the room I have been calling a lounge, but apparently it is a solarium. I am not sure exactly how many windows a lounge has to have to make it a solarium. This one has a lot, but I guess I sort of thought a solarium needed a glass roof or at least a skylight. What the hell do I know?

There is no one watching Hong Kong comedies this time, but there is another guy in there. He looks over at us, but we studiously ignore him. I don't feel like having to make conversation with a stranger right now.

Kirsten and I laugh and make jokes, and the cute nurse comes back and tells us that Phlebotomy is on their way and that we probably will get dismissed again to get lunch. After she leaves, Kirsten says, "You know, every time they say 'Phlebotomy' now, I start singing it to the tune of 'Teenage Lobotomy' . . . Phleboto-my! Phleboto-my!"

The other guy in the lounge is snoozing, but eventually he stirs and forces the issue by saying, "Ugh . . . so lazy. I worked all night."

"Oh, yeah, that's tough," we reply.

"Came here at 6:00 for my dad. He has leukemia." I make some kind of sympathetic noise, and Kirsten says that she is in for breast cancer. He replies, "Yeah, I had two aunts die of breast cancer."

It is all I can do not to sarcastically praise him for his smooth conversational salvo. Hey, that's great, thanks for sharing that information. Ever hear of anyone who got better, Dr. Kevorkian?

He then busts out with, "Are you Catholic?" I can't imagine where he's going with this, but I am sure it can't be good, but before Kirsten can sputter out a reply, the phlebotomist comes in right on cue and draws two vials out of Kirsten's arm, and we head off to lunch.

Kirsten, who is in every way a better person than me (except, maybe, for her lamentable fondness for that James Taylor *Great-*

est Hits record), says at the elevators, "Oh, he probably was going to offer to pray for me or something." I suggest that he didn't need to know if you were Catholic to offer his prayers—I think he was going to recommend some kind of ritual involving either a saint or some holy place or substance.

As the elevator goes down, we get quiet for a minute, then Kirsten says, "I hope this works."

"It will," I tell her. It had fucking well better.

We do not go back to the brewpub place, but rather to the same Mexican place Rowen and I went to the night when Kirsten supposedly had heart-stopping levels of potassium in her blood. The food is still excellent, and we trudge back to the hospital and sit in her room for two hours waiting for a surgeon to come put a hose in her. At some point a resident comes in and gives Kirsten some kind of neural checkup that involves her doing things that look a lot like stuff Moe does to Curly in Three Stooges movies, only without the hitting or that satisfying hollow "Bonk!" It gets so ridiculous that when she asks Kirsten to puff out her cheeks I say, "Is there a medical reason for this, or are you just having fun with us?"

Clearly this woman has no future in the medical profession, because she can actually take a joke, and she laughs and tells us yes, these are real tests they do to see if the chemo has fried your brain or not. Kirsten's brain is, happily, unfried.

I have to leave to pick up Rowen before the surgeon shows up, so I miss the bedside surgery ritual. I go home first. The car is still there. I park on the street and run inside and call parking enforcement again. "Oh, yeah," the guy says in a bored voice, "well, we'll try to get somebody out there." I hold out no hope at all that this car is ever going to get moved. I start thinking that if I ever commit a crime, I will just park my car across someone's driveway and hide in it, since it seems to be a surefire way to avoid any attention at all from the authorities.

I pick Rowen up and she immediately starts crying, "I want mommy . . . I want mommy . . ." I hug her and say, "Me too."

We go out to dinner, back to the same place we went with my mom and Kirsten's parents the night I frantically called Kirsten from the bathroom. Rowen is cheery as we eat our bread, and she tells me awesome four-year-old knock-knock jokes involving items on the table, like, "Knock knock."

"Who's there?"

"Noodle."

"Noodle who?"

"Noodle salt shaker!" We laugh uproariously at these and the people next to us look at me like I'm a total moron, or at least an incredibly annoying cutesy parent. Maybe I am. I don't care.

We then play this game where she pretends to knock on my door and I say, "Who is it?"

And she replies, "It's me, your friend!"

"Hi friend! Thanks for coming over! Did you bring any bacon?"

"Oh yes—here it is," and she hands me a piece of noodle or a bit of bread. We do this for probably fifteen minutes. I should add that Rowen has never had bacon in her life.

Our waitress is very cool about us hanging around for a long time and goes out of her way to be nice to Rowen, and I end up leaving her a huge tip (well, okay, five bucks, but that seems huge to me on a fifteen-dollar check) because I always try to overtip when the servers are nice to Rowen in hopes that it will encourage more of them to be nice to kids, instead of trying half-heartedly to disguise their annoyance when you show up with them.

The other good thing is that they seem to have finally canned the depressive John Hiatt wannabe guitar player, and the piano player is back doing instrumental versions of "Makin' Whoopee," "Ain't Misbehavin'," and some Beatles numbers, and it makes it very pleasant to hang out there, as opposed to feeling like you are eavesdropping on someone's therapy appointment.

It is freezing cold and raining, which is probably the most depressing weather there is, but Rowen is happy and so am I. When we get home, the car that was blocking our driveway is gone.

Tumblin' Dice

This round of high-dose chemo proves to be a lot easier to take than the first one. Kirsten doesn't puke at all, so they don't have to keep her high as a kite to fight the nausea. Also, for some reason they are allowing her to have her door open and walk down to the solarium this time, which seems to make a big difference. It's not really much of a walk or much of a change of scene—just a tiny lounge with other sick people in johnnies—but it beats the hell out of the same room for three weeks.

I go to see her and she doesn't really seem much worse than when she had those initial doses of regular chemo—a little tired, but also cheerful and not completely worn out like she was before.

All of this is good news. So why am I so depressed?

Well, I guess I realize that I now have to shift emotional and mental gears again. Kirsten got her last dose of chemo yesterday. So she still needs to get stem cells again and everything, but in terms of her getting medicine to fight her cancer, we're done. And I am terrified.

While this whole treatment has not been easy at all, it has been kind of okay emotionally to be in the thick of the battle and feel like we are really doing all we can to fight it. And now it's just upsetting to realize that the treatment is over. They have used everything in their arsenal. There's no more medicine to wait for: first it was, "Well, when they hit it with the big dose, that will really get it," and then it was, "Well, when we get the second dose, that's going to be the big left-right combination that sends the cancer to the mat for good," and now it's, "Well, we'll wait a couple of weeks and see what happens and see how well this worked." I am just not mentally prepared to have that information yet if it's anything at all except complete victory against the cancer.

I still hope and believe that she is going to beat this, but I am so scared, so scared of losing her. And right now it seems like we have rolled the dice, and we just have to wait and see what comes up.

This dice metaphor floats around in my head for about thirty seconds before it picks up the Rolling Stones' "Tumblin' Dice," which has been playing nonstop on my mental jukebox for about three days, and I must confess that I've never listened very closely to the words, so it may be about something completely different, though from the words I do remember it doesn't seem to be about much of anything, but anyway I don't even own a copy of *Exile on Main Street* to go check. I recognize this as a gaping hole in my record collection. It is particularly problematic right now, because when I get a song stuck in my head, actually hearing it is the only way to exorcise it, which is why I bought that Stooges album.

Exile on Main Street is, if I remember correctly from reading about it and examining Danny's copy, the album they made where they all holed up in a French château for some long period of time and wrote and recorded the album there, and you can just tell from the photo on the sleeve of Mick and Keith laying down vocals and at least one of them has a half-empty bottle of bourbon in his hand that it was probably a debauch of really epic proportions, and of course that leads me to the great cosmic joke of Kirsten being sick while Keith Fucking Richards is this healthy old man, but mostly it makes me want to hole up in some French château with all my friends and a bunch of booze and groupies, and even if I didn't end up producing one of the greatest records ever, well, it sure sounds like a hell of a vacation.

How It Ends

I have been thinking a lot about how this book ends, and I need to confess to you right now that I think I may disappoint you. Because, of course, what you want, if you are at all like me, is a real ending. I always hate movies and books that just stop rather than ending, or that get cutesy with the end. I read *Infinite Jest*, all eight thousand pages of it or whatever, and then the fucking thing just stops and doesn't tie up any of the plot lines you've been following for 7,999 pages, and you keep reading through to page 8,000 because you care about the characters and the situation, and then the author basically spits on you for being chump enough to care about the characters and situations and says, "No no no—view this novel with ironic detachment and appreciate on an intellectual level how clever I am!"

When I was in college I was persuaded by my pre-Kirsten girlfriend to read *The French Lieutenant's Woman,* and you can tell I was infatuated and eager to please her since I read a post-modern take on a Victorian novel, basically combining my two most hated genres in one book, and, there again, same deal. I got all wrapped up in the stupid romance, will he or she marry below his or her station or whatever it always is in these insufferable books, and then it has three different endings. Oooh, that's deep, man. People still read this book (largely, I think because Meryl Streep looks really fetching in that cloak on the cover) and think it's great that this guy abdicated the author's job, which is to pick an ending.

All of which is to say, I feel your pain. Here are my three possible endings:

Ending one: Complete remission.
This, I guess, is the happy ending. No guarantees, of course, but we can pretty much get on with the business of trying to put our life back together without having to worry, at least for a period of time, about treatments and tests and whatnot. Maybe it comes back, maybe it doesn't, but we get to relax for a while.

Ending two: Partial remission.
I have no idea if that's even a real medical term. I guess it must be—since they throw "complete remission" around, that pretty much implies that there exists something less than complete remission, otherwise to call it complete is redundant. Anyway, this ending, I think, bites. Maybe. This ending means more treatments, followed by more treatments, leading up to more treatments . . . you get the idea. I guess there will still be breathers in there, and I will continue to believe that, you know, she will respond really well to Herceptin, or those new tumor-starving drugs will be perfected, and basically that I still get to have Kirsten for a long long time. And I am sure that there will still be gladness and joy in that time, because she makes me happy and I try to do the same for her, and I know Rowen cracks us both up on a daily basis, but I guess we'll be all about fighting cancer forever.

Ending three: They all die.
Okay, now I'm getting cute. This is the ending of *The Unbearable Lightness of Being,* the movie anyway, I never read the book,

I know, I know, it's magical and lyrical and I really should read it, but I am trying to read only things with exploding heads and/or lesbian vampires for the time being, but the movie was this three-hour snooze fest in which Daniel Day-Lewis has hot adulterous sex in the first twenty mintues and spends the rest of the movie not having enough adulterous sex to make the damn thing interesting, but too much for his wife's taste, and somewhere in the second hour the Russians roll into Prague, which I guess was some kind of metaphor I was too stupid to get, and then he keeps cheating, and just as you're wondering if they are ever going to figure their relationship out and whether you are ever going to care, they die in a car crash.

They all die. That is the ending, really. It's everybody's ending, and we are all fooling ourselves if we think it's not. So whatever we do or do not know about Kirsten's death, we know it's inevitable. So is mine. So, I'm sorry to say, is yours.

My hope is that whatever happens, we can reach some kind of peace with this idea. That we don't have to have some imaginary guarantee that we get to see our grandchildren get married or whatever, but that we can just get up tomorrow and do our thing and love each other and laugh and have sex and say at the end of the day, like Ice Cube, "It was a good day."

Unlike John Fowles's *French Lieutenant's Woman,* I promise to pick an ending, but what sucks is that I will not be able to tell you, "Now we know for sure that she's beaten it forever." And if that sucks for you, believe me that it sucks a whole lot more for me.

Fat Boys

I have sold a lot of records at used record stores, and I only have two regrets. One was that in the ninth grade I sold my copy of AC/DC's *Back in Black* because I had liked it in the seventh grade and I was so beyond that. (I bought it again four years later. No harm done, except I was out several bucks on the deal.) And the other one is that I sold the first Fat Boys album with the long song about them going to jail because they broke into the grocery store to steal a midnight snack. Sigh. The album is now out of print and probably some kind of collector's item, and it just can't be had for love or money.

It's okay, because I am now becoming one of the Fat Boys. Admittedly I have not swelled to Human Beat Box proportions, but I am getting large in the gut and breasts. I can still hide it pretty well under my clothes, and I haven't had to go over a 34 waist yet, but with my shirt off—well, I have a larger belly than I'd like and quite an impressive rack.

I guess it's a healthy sign that I am concerned enough about this to want to do something about it. I mean, part of it is that, you know, it's winter, and it's harder to exercise as much, and I basically do a lot of staying inside and eating in the winter, but really it's all about the sweets.

See, I am a sweets addict. And I need to go cold turkey. I am only half joking here. I mean, I do go days without sweets, and I have never lied to cover up my sweets addiction, and my loved ones have not arranged an intervention. But the bottom line is that it is much much easier for me to have no cookies than to have one. Now I could not sit down and eat a whole bag of Oreos, but I will eat maybe eight. I will eat them until I feel disgusting or the supply runs out, whichever comes first.

Brownies, muffins, same deal. It's really all about the baked goods with me rather than candy. And so in this time of high stress (not to mention four children's birthday parties in the space of five weeks), I have turned back to sweets as a stress reducer.

It's not working. Now I'm just stressed out and fat.

After my dad died, everybody brought over food—tons and tons of food for weeks and weeks, and I got the message that food comforts you, food is your friend, and now it still is, except it's not a very good friend, so it's time for me to say goodbye. (Yes, alcohol has a lot of calories too, and giving up beer and wine would probably help too, but I can't give up all my phony stress reducers, now can I?)

I have been trying for a week and have lost two pounds. Of course, that was on two different scales, so it might just be a calibration difference.

I sure hope we get good news about this treatment. I don't know if I can resist the siren song of the double chocolate muffins if we don't.

That Lonesome Valley

One night I dream that Kirsten and I are in the hospital, and we are both getting chemo. Suddenly I have this moment where I realize—hey, wait a minute! Do I have cancer? I immediately check my testicles. No . . . I rack my brains trying to remember what part of my body it's in. And then I realize that I don't have cancer at all. So what am I doing here getting chemo?

This is the thought that wakes me up, and I lie there in the dark, confused in that just-woke-from-a-weird-dream kind of way. Eventually I realize that no, I don't have cancer. I guess this is my subconscious trying to tell me that I feel like I am having this same experience, that, you know, as Sam and Dave said, when something is wrong with my baby, something is wrong with me.

And while this is true to a certain extent, it also is not true in a pretty important way. I worry about Kirsten, I sleep like shit, I eat too much, but the bottom line is that I'm not sick. And she is. And I can't be where she is. I have felt this very keenly at times—sometimes in the early days after the diagnosis, or after a particularly bad piece of news, Kirsten would be kind of withdrawn, or just depressed, and I would try so hard to cheer her up that I would just be annoying, and I realized that she is just in a place where I'm not. I can imagine what it's like being there, but I'm not there, and she is.

I think about this when she is in the hospital. As I leave her in her room with the chemo pumping into her veins, she seems very alone to me. Even when I am sitting next to her, I am not with her. She is fighting for her life, and while, you know, I can sort of be the Burgess Meredith character in the corner, she is the one trying to go the distance with Apollo Creed.

The Carter Family, of course, have a song that speaks directly to this whole thing. It's called "Lonesome Valley," and it goes:

> *Everybody's got to walk*
> *That lonesome valley*
> *They got to walk*
> *It by themselves*
> *There's nobody here*
> *Can walk it for them*
> *They got to walk*
> *It by themselves.*

It then goes on to substitute "my mother," "my father," and something unintelligible for "everybody." As usual, they are right on target. I suppose what they are really talking about is that you ultimately have to die alone. But I also take it to mean that when you are suffering, when you are struggling, you have to do it by yourself. It says on the back of the CD that this cheerful little number was a top ten hit for them, which just goes to show you that the pop charts were a very very different place in the 1930s.

So Kirsten has to walk that lonesome valley by herself. If it was me, I would be thinking constantly about death. I don't really know what she thinks of—I guess when she is in the midst of treatment it is pretty easy to just focus on the moment—now my muscles ache like hell, now I have to puke—and not worry about eternity. But I know she is scared sometimes; she is living most people's worst nightmare.

I think about this as I walk down the corridor inside the bone marrow transplant bubble ward one day and see all the patients there in their johnnies. Most doors are open, and most of the people are in bed, but I look in at all these people and think, well, they got up this morning. They are walking that lonesome valley by themselves, and most people live in fear of being where these people are, but they got up today, and they are doing it, and that lady who was on oxygen yesterday isn't today, and while some of these people won't make it and others will walk out of here and be well for decades, today I feel, and I know that this sounds like the kind of cheesy, facile, inspirational crap I have been mocking for months, inspired by all these bald people in blue johnnies. I know secondhand how fucking hard this is, and when I see a guy shuffle down the hallway just to look out the window, I just think well, shit, there goes a superhero. And this doesn't make me think, oh well, I should really appreciate what I have or anything like that, it does not for a second give me any perspective because I am a self-centered shit, but it does make me proud to be a human. Whatever it is that lets these people get up and eat their awful hospital food and shuffle down the hallways and live every day, you and I have it too—we must, because I don't for a second believe this well-meaning bullshit that several people have shoveled my way about how God only gives us what we can handle. What about the people who are tortured to death and die screaming? Is God up there figuring, well, a certain number of broom handles need to get inserted into rectums today, so I will pick only the people who are strong enough to handle it? I don't know much about God, but I sure don't want to believe in one that operates that way.

So I don't believe that these people's diseases hovered around looking for somebody who could handle being sick. They are people like you and me who are sick. Today these people are not scary and pathetic to me (though they might well be tomorrow and they sure as hell were yesterday). Today they are superheroes, not because they are special, but because they aren't.

Exile on My Street

So I go out and buy a copy of *Exile on Main Street* within a few days of obsessing about "Tumblin' Dice," and when I get the CD I am disappointed to see that the song is referred to everywhere as "Tumbling Dice," which just seems kind of odd because Mick never says the "g," and if you pronounce the name of the song with the "g" on it, it just sounds dorky. I still have no fucking idea what that song is about. Ironically, my mom calls me while I am in the record store, and we have a nice conversation, mostly, and she says that since I am in the record store, I should buy her this other CD she wants to make up for the one I stole from her, and I sort of consider it, but I laugh and say no way. She is trying hard, but I still don't feel guilty. Not sure why.

The rest of the record is good, but I am not sure it's as amazingly mindbendingly good as everybody says it is. The song that catches my attention most at first is "Rocks Off," which leads off the record and in which Mick complains that he only gets his rocks off when he's sleeeeeeeeepin, and given the state of my life right now I can sympathize, even though I find it hard to believe that that was ever really a problem for Mick, who, if you believe what you read (and you know I do when it comes to celebrity gossip), has gotten his rocks off more or less every twenty minutes for the last forty years or so. I mention this to Danny on the phone, and he confesses that he shared my puzzlement, and finally concluded that Mick is not talking about actual ejaculation, but just basically saying that the thing he really most enjoys is sleeping. Given the state of my life right now, I sympathize with that interpretation too.

We get to have Kirsten home for a few days. She definitely seems much better than she did after her first megadose and stem cell transplant. Nan is here helping out, and she does stuff like the daily cleaning that I am too feeble to do and takes Kirsten to "day camp" at the hospital. She has to go in every day to get fluids and get blood drawn and tested, and they tell her that if she spikes a fever of 100.5, she is back in for ten days.

I love having Kirsten here rather than in the hospital, and Nan is really the perfect helper (and now seems like a good time to give a shout out to her husband and three kids, who go spouse- and mom-less for ten days while she's here, and her mother-in-law, who flies down to Louisiana to stay with them while Nan is up here), and I am sullen as hell. Part of this is just being nervous about what's coming up, and part of it is that Kirsten deteriorates every day she's home, and it's just hard to have her be so sick. Except for her forays into day camp, she basically camps out on the couch, and drinks lots of fluids and eats less each day, and I know this is just the treatment and not the disease, but it makes me sad to see her like this.

It is also a weird week at work because the students are all gone doing internships at local radio stations, government offices, hospitals, etc. I guess it's a nice opportunity for them, and it is also sort of nice to have some time to do those things I have been meaning to do but haven't gotten around to, and none of the meetings we have are too painful, but the bottom line is that I didn't get into teaching to hang around with grown-ups all day. It's draining. It's also depressing, because the pace is much slower than normal, so I have lots of time to just ponder how fucked up my life is right now. One of my co-workers announces that she is pregnant, and she is a lovely woman and will be a great mom, and I want to be happy for her, but I am an evil little gnome, and all I am is jealous that other people have things to be happy about, while my big news is that Kirsten is officially neutropenic, which means she has basically no white blood cells, and did I mention that we are waiting to find out if this treatment that almost killed her has worked or not?

One day I am sad all day because I had a dream about being in some kind of funeral home looking at urns and touring crematoriums or something. The dream carries the emotional reality of the terrible horror of going through all that funeral shit, and I have a bad dream hangover all day, and I just feel sad, and there are no kids to make me think about anything else, just piles of shit on my desk that represent stuff I haven't done because I didn't want to do it.

I decide that after Nan leaves, I will take care of Rowen by myself. I have taken her to school early a few days, admittedly with mixed results, but I am optimistic. She refuses to spend much time with anybody else in the evening, and I can go visit Kirsten in the hospital during the day, so it doesn't make a lot of sense to have anybody else here. Also, as much as it is helpful to have people here, it is also kind of exhausting. You just never really get to relax when someone else is in your space.

My decision goes over like a lead balloon with both sets of parents. My mom offers on the phone, "Oh. Well, that's a pretty long day for Rowen," and I say, "Thanks for your input," and she gives me one of these things where she is yelling but sort of laughing and saying that it's not like she's so controlling and she does have some expertise to share, you know. And I know that she wants to feel valued and useful, and who doesn't, but I try to explain that when she says something like "that's a long day for her" as though I haven't considered it, it really doesn't come across as sharing expertise.

Nan breaks the news to Kirsten's mom (well, her mom too)—on Saturday they are coming up to take Nan and Rowen to lunch while I take Kirsten to day camp. Day camp totally blows. It is boring as hell, and Kirsten is content to just space out or snooze. We watch several cooking shows on TV, including one where this woman makes this incredible over-the-top dish that involves cooking in a tomato sauce the following items: sausages, meatballs, and beef stuffed with prosciutto. I just about hork right there.

When we get back from day camp, Kirsten's mom is sitting on

the couch. She says that Nan, Rowen, and Kirsten's dad went out to lunch and she, inexplicably, stayed here. They stay gone for about another hour, and Kirsten's mom says almost nothing during that time. Clearly she is pissed about something, but neither Kirsten nor I has the energy to drag it out of her, so I just sort of assume it's the news she got about me wanting to go it alone.

I get sort of bummed out wondering if our relationships with our parents are going to survive this whole thing. Right now, though, I am really more worried about whether Kirsten is going to survive this whole thing, so I guess I will go on gleefully offending everybody and hope they forgive me for it later.

Kirsten is in pretty bad shape after we get home from day camp—not emotionally, just physically. Her temperature climbs from 99.1 to 99.9 to 100.1. I remember the last time Nan was here and Kirsten's temperature climbed slowly over the course of a day, and I am convinced that it will hit 100.5 and she will need to go in again, and this upsets me, because as hard as it is having her here sick, it is harder to not have her here at all for ten days. Every time I haul out the thermometer, though, Kirsten says, "I'm not going in tonight. I've got one more night at home." She is right. She crashes at about seven o'clock, and I shove a thermometer into her mouth before letting her sleep. Her temperature is 99.9. Reprieved, she heads off to bed. Knowing I won't have to drive, I pour myself a glass of wine, pop a movie in the VCR, and watch with joy as the Toxic Avenger deals gruesome death to the evildoers of Tromaville.

Another One Bites the Dust

Kirsten eventually spikes a fever and goes back into the hospital on Sunday, and Nan leaves on Tuesday. My tenure as a single parent does not have an auspicious beginning. I do an okay job getting Rowen off to school and putting dinner on the table at night, and getting her bathed and tucked in and everything, and then in the middle of the night on Tuesday, mind you I have been on the job on my own for less than a day, Rowen starts crying and complaining that her stomach hurts. She has been known to malinger in the middle of the night, but as I talk to her I am convinced that she is really in pain. Of course the first thing I think of is how that kid from *Poltergeist* died after going into the hospital with stomach pains, because that is just how my mind works, but I convince myself it's probably gas, brought on in part by the apple she had for dinner. I put her in a warm bath (at 12:30 A.M.!), hoping that it will move things along, and sure enough, as soon as she gets out she hops on the toilet and does a rather spectacular poo.

I am pretty proud of myself for being so resourceful. She goes back to bed, and I am almost back to sleep when I hear this "Ack! Ack!" and I run into her room and she has puked all over her sheets. So I strip the bed and wipe it out of her hair and it is just a terrible scene, because she pukes again twenty minutes later, and then again, and then again, and so on from 12:30 until 4:00. Because I am not thinking clearly, I don't just put clothes on and get up—each time she finishes, I figure, well, she's got to be done now and go back to bed, and then just as we are both almost back to sleep, she pukes again. We both stay home the next day and in spite of it all end up having a pretty good time together. She has made a complete recovery by about 7:00 A.M., and we have a funny scene as she is sucking down orange juice and munching Cheerios and I am on the phone with the nurse at her pediatrician's office, and she is telling me, "Keep her off of solid foods until dinnertime. Water and apple juice are okay, but no citrus juices." This is the second time in a week I have flouted medical advice. Last week Rowen had her yearly checkup, and I had to wrestle her while she screamed bloody murder to get her to be moderately still when they took her blood, so when they called me to tell me her cholesterol was elevated and we needed to have her do a fasting test because the test is really not accurate, I said no way, we don't eat meat and she won't drink milk and didn't you just say the test isn't accurate, and they pushed me, so I played the cancer card and they stopped.

Kirsten's mom ends up coming up that day so that I can have some time to see Kirsten in the hospital. Whatever weirdness was going on before seems to have passed, and I really do appreciate having her here—I needed help, and she provided it.

That night after Rowen has gone to bed, Kirsten's mom is reading a mystery novel (this one is part of a series with a mystery-antiques connection, not to be confused with the many different series with a mystery-cat connection, though I wouldn't swear that there's no cat living in the antique store) and I am playing video games, when the phone rings. It is my mom, and she informs me that my grandfather is dead.

This news means nothing to me. Not because I hate the guy, but because he is just nothing to me. He left his family when my mom was nine, and this was actually kind of a relief from his alcoholism and abuse, and to say he was not close with his children is a tremendous understatement. I saw him a handful of times at family gatherings where he was always either actively annoying or slightly out of it, except for the one time when he and my uncle got in a fistfight for reasons too stupid to get into, but all you need to know about the man's popularity among his descendants is that I was standing next to two of my cousins when the fight broke out between their father and grandfather, and I still remember them whispering through clenched teeth, "Get him, dad! Get him!"

So I console my mom a little bit because she is upset, though she kind of can't figure out why because, as she says, she's not going to miss him and she doesn't really care that he's dead, and that may sound harsh, but given the stories I have heard, the guy will be lucky if there's not a conga line across his grave.

We talk for a few minutes, and I go back to playing my video game, because I had almost figured out how to rescue the two . . . well, never mind.

I keep turning the conversation over in my mind, and I realize what a total shit I've been regarding both my mom and Kirsten's parents. My mom is sad because she doesn't care that her father is dead, and I think, well, shit, as much as this whole thing has been a strain on all of our relationships, the bottom line is that they love us a lot and they are doing the best they can for us, and maybe I should be a little bit less persnickety about whether they are always doing everything exactly the way I want them to. I mean, just being able to say that they love us and are doing their best for us is something that my mom was never able to say about her father, and something I guess a lot of people can never say. It's a tremendous gift, and I feel bad for having looked askance at it even for a second.

The Waiting

Kirsten's time in the hospital passes pretty uneventfully, and after the puke disaster, I am able to take care of Rowen by myself for an entire week until she comes home. A few good things start happening: one is that Kirsten is starting to get peach fuzz on her head. The first time I notice this, she is in the hospital and pumped full of morphine and not in the greatest shape, but it makes me feel really hopeful. It is weird hair, though—really soft, literally like peach fuzz, and not at all like the hard stubble that portends real hair growth. I am not sure if it will fall out and make way for real stubble or what. I am also not sure, but I think it's no longer red but, rather, white.

God, or whoever controls the weather, is nice enough to give us a snow day on the day Kirsten is scheduled to be released. This means I get to go pick her up, and this is really nice. Kirsten's mom then stays with us for a few days, and this turns out to be basically devoid of tension.

I start playing puzzle games on the PlayStation. In some pathetic way I think this signals that my brain is returning from vacation.

The kids come back to school and I remember once again why I love my job. Two weeks with no kids is really too long to keep a bunch of teachers cooped up together. By the end we were all worked up about a bunch of stupid petty crap, and people were snapping at each other in meetings. My conclusion from all this is that I am not the only one who prefers the company of teenagers to adults during the workday. And, if I am honest, I guess I have to say that most of us also prefer being the center of attention all day, which gets difficult in meetings, so we take turns speechifying and/or having tantrums just to make sure we get a piece of that spotlight we usually have all day long and crave to an unseemly degree.

And so now Kirsten is home, and once again she is tired and mostly stays on the couch, but she makes incremental improvements, and I know that she will be her old self in a matter of weeks.

Perversely, this sends me into an emotional tailspin. I become completely grumpy, and my grumpiness is relieved only by teaching, and occasionally by spending time with Rowen. (I have to say that while picking her up from school is usually pleasant, and I am able to forget everything while she trudges up the side of a snowbank shouting, "I have to climb the mountain of mange!" taking her to school is not exactly the idyllic bonding experience I thought it would be and is actually kind of a pain in the ass because you just can't get a four-year-old to get hip to the idea of a tight schedule. The one day we make it out of the house kind of early and I am encouraged about the time, she begins shuffling along the sidewalk [like Tim Conway when he played the old guy who always frustrated Harvey Korman's impatient customer on *The Carol Burnett Show*] because she is afraid that walking at a normal speed will cause her shoes to come untied. I end up carrying her, which does horrible things to my back for three days.)

The immediate crisis of treatment and hospitalization is over, and in some ways, crisis mode is a little easier because there is no time to think. Get up, get Rowen to school, go to work, go to the hospital, pay way too much for coffee, visit with Kirsten, come back to work, pick Rowen up, make dinner, put Rowen to bed, watch something inane on TV for twenty minutes, and collapse into bed. Now that that frantic pace has subsided, I once again have time to think, and I hate thinking. What if, what if, what if. I am relieved that treatment is over, but what if she really is going to need more? What if that becomes our life? What if this disease takes her away from me soon? Whatever happens, how the hell are we supposed to live?

I have no idea, and I am sort of depressed that I don't feel like I've been transformed by this experience at all. I haven't had any great spiritual revelation, I haven't learned to live each day and take it as it comes, I have not found any peace or serenity. Sometimes when Rowen is having a tantrum she will say, "I hate everything! I want to smash the whole world!" This is kind of how I feel all the time now. I guess I should be praying or meditating or something, in fact I think that's what I need to do to try to figure out how to live, but it just sounds so fucking boring. Right now I am feeling much too nihilistic for spiritual contemplation—I feel like I'd much rather go on a three-day bender and go get drunk with strippers or something.

I'm sure most strippers are really stimulating conversationalists, and probably adore short, grumpy high school teachers with big guts, so this is probably an excellent plan. I'll see you in three days.

The fact is that I just don't know how to live anymore. Even if we do get good news when we get news about this treatment. I ask Kirsten when her next appointment is one day, and she says, "I have no idea. Dr. J is in fucking Africa."

"Is she at some sort of conference or something?" (This has happened before—one of the downsides of having a hotshot doc.)

"No. She's on sa*fa*ri!"

"Is it a surfin' safari?"

"I don't think they do much surfin' in Kenya. I think it's one of those photo safaris."

"But they might do some, right? I mean, you don't know that it's *not* a surfin' safari."

"Yes," she says finally, rolling her eyes so as to show it's just easier to give in, "it's a surfin' safari."

So whenever Dr. J gets back from her surfin' safari, we'll find out how the treatment worked. And then what? Kirsten's death will always be hanging over us, and this makes it much harder for me to ignore the fact that my death, and the death of everyone I care about, is inevitable and could strike at any time. How the hell do you live like this?

I guess you just do what the people in the blue johnnies over on the bubble floor do. You just get up every day and do it, and you try like hell not to think about it too much. My experience in crisis mode confirms this. Life is easy when you just get up and do it every day. It is the waiting and worrying that make it hard. Robert Burns's "To a Mouse," which is famous for that line about how the best-laid schemes of mice and men gang aft agley, not oft go awry, you can look it up, ends with him saying to the mouse, yeah, you know, I wrecked your house with the plow and I'm sorry, but you still have it better than me because you can just live in the moment, whereas "forward . . . I guess an' fear!"

But then, mice get squashed or eat poison and rarely get to attend their grandchildren's weddings. And sometimes, if "Froggy Went a-Courtin' " is to be believed, they marry outside the species anyway. I have no idea where I'm going with this. To bed, I guess.

What I've Learned

I was feeling bad about the fact that after going through a life-changing trauma, I don't feel that I have learned anything, so I decided to list everything I've learned in the last five months. Here goes:

I eat too much.

I have four alcoholic cousins. The disease carries on, and I need to be very careful in this area.

In a crisis, people will surprise you with their amazing kindness. This is particularly true of people you don't know especially well and are not related to. I mean, someone I work with and have had lots of conflicts with (he's one of the people my smart, trouble-making advisees can't stop mouthing off to) went and spent two hours donating platelets. What did I ever do to deserve this kindness from him?

In a crisis, people will get on your nerves. I have given numerous examples of this, but it was driven home to me as my mom recounted stories of her and her siblings all biting each other's heads off around every stupid little detail of their father's funeral.

Coffee is a wonderful gift from God. Really. Getting coffee when I went to visit Kirsten in the hospital made it semifestive, and going to get coffee (for me, and a bagel for her) has been a nice excuse for Rowen and me to get out of the house and just be somewhere else. When I saw dying people's friends and relatives in the bubble ward, they would inevitably be clutching cups of coffee or else sending somebody to go get cups of coffee. It is just a wonderful source of comfort.

I am at my best as a parent when we are out of the house. I don't know why this is, but Rowen and I have a great time going to the coffee shop, or the grocery store, or wherever. It is effortless fun, whereas if we are stuck in the house on a rainy day or whatever, I have no idea how to entertain her. I am in awe of people like our friend Jen who, given about ten seconds and two glue sticks, can come up with an art or craft project that will entertain a kid for an hour.

Today's youth don't, despite what I said earlier, relish the impossibility of today's video games—they cheat. The games, I have learned, are written with these built-in codes, freely available on the Internet, that allow you to have infinite lives, or disable all opponents, or whatever. There's also an actual device you can buy that will save you from the tedium of figuring out the game and the tedium of looking for cheat codes on the Internet and just automatically cheat for you. Maybe they should just make the games easier.

Exile on Main Street, despite what I said earlier, is as good as everybody says it is.

Though this is counterintuitive, facing a real trauma seems to be a pretty good cure for hypochondria. During this whole ordeal I have been able to serenely ignore a variety of aches and pains that, in the past, would have kept me awake at night. I guess the real crisis was just taking up all the mental energy I usually spend on phantom illnesses.

Music is the closest thing I have found to evidence of God's existence. While it is important for many Christians to believe that Christ was human and felt our pain, for me it's important that Hank Williams was human and felt our pain. I don't mean to suggest that the abusive, substance-abusing elder Mr. Williams was in any way Christlike, but the next time you feel really shitty, go listen to "I'm So Lonesome I Could Cry." He is singing your story. (Hank left us some great gifts. Of course, he also, however unintentionally, inflicted the music of Hank Williams Jr. on the world, so I guess the scales are about even in terms of his legacy.) Or take the Clash, or Johnny Cash, the Carter Family, whatever—music is the only thing that has really made me feel, in a deep way I can believe, that we are not alone down here.

Hire a professional to do your pest control. I paid through

the nose to get some pros to take care of our mice, but they made the traps and poison invisible and I haven't seen a mouse since, and it was worth every cent to not have to smash the little bastards myself.

Most of all, Kirsten is just my favorite person on earth.

Freedom

The fact remains that teaching is a really sweet gig, and three weeks after the kids come back from their sojourn in the work world, we all go on vacation for a week. For some reason, schools in New England have a vacation in February and another one in April, instead of one in March, which is what we had growing up in Ohio, and this makes absolutely no sense to me. I mean, on the one hand, February is probably the shittiest month of the year, and it is nice to have a break during that time. On the other hand, having a week off in the shittiest month of the year is not so very great if you don't have the wherewithal to, say, fly to Aruba. Mostly you stay inside.

After work on Friday, I go with some co-workers to a bar near school where many people go after work, and I really enjoy being with these people. I am reminded once again of how lucky I am. In other places I worked, I was occasionally forced to socialize with my co-workers and usually wanted to run screaming from the room, so this is a nice change.

While we are sitting at the bar, Wham!'s "Freedom," which may be their best work, and which I haven't heard in years, and which you inexplicably hear much much less often than some of their lesser tunes, comes on, and I begin bobbing my head, and when some of my co-workers begin to mock me and the song, I feel that I have to set them straight and explain that this is an almost perfect pop song.

Vacation begins. Kirsten and I do naughty things like go out for coffee and lunch before getting a medical okay to do such things, and vow to remain silent about these activities when we see Dr. J on Wednesday. I rent *Willy Wonka and the Chocolate Factory* to watch with Rowen, and as we're watching, I just start to cry. It is one of the first movies I ever saw, and one of only two movies I remember seeing with just my father, and it just makes me so happy to now be the dad watching this with my little kid that I sit there with tears running down my cheeks as Augustus Gloop goes ass-over-teakettle into the chocolate river.

I go for a walk up to the park and stumble on something really strange and cool—what appear to be abandoned animal enclosures. I am on the other end of the park from where the zoo is now, but there are zoo ruins up here—giant stone enclosures enclosed by the ghosts of metal bars, mostly rusted away. For some reason I don't understand and therefore can't explain, this just entrances me—I feel like I am ten years old again, and all I can do is say, "Cooooooooooool!" It is cool and eerie in the way that all ruins are, and it is a site for illegal nocturnal partying in the way that all ruined structures in urban areas are, as the crack pipe I find on the ground attests.

I have been feeling like a Zen master again, which probably means I am due for a bout of depression, but I am enjoying each day while it lasts. Petey takes me out for a beer the night before

Kirsten's big follow-up appointment with Dr. J and remarks on the fact that I seem really calm and happy, and I tell him that I had a wonderful day today. Maybe tomorrow is going to suck, but today didn't. Kirsten and I lingered over coffee, I watched this wonderfully demented and emotionally significant movie with Rowen, I found zoo ruins, and here I am having a beer with a friend—it's pretty close to a perfect day. While I wish to God I could feel like this every day, I know that I will get depressed again, and things will piss me off, but ultimately I think a day like this here and there is just about all any of us can hope for. I don't know if it's denial or if it is just serene living in the moment. I'm no longer sure that there's much of a difference. I mean, sure, some terrible fate may be waiting for Kirsten, or me, or all of us, but it didn't happen today. People talk about denial like it's a bad thing, but I don't know—what the fuck are we supposed to do, walk around looking like Droopy all day, going, "Woe is me"? I can never really forget about it, but I also don't have to think about it all the time—like I said, maybe enjoying today is some kind of denial, because I am not processing my potential grief or my fear or whatever, but I am fucking tired of doing that shit. I just want to have a nice day. And I do! And I think, if I'm lucky, I will have more. And like I said, there are no guarantees, so I think this is just about all any of us can ask for out of life.

The next day Kirsten and I drop Rowen off at preschool and go over to see Dr. J, who has returned from her surfin' safari. We have a long appointment which does not give us very much actual news but is very comforting. Basically it turns out that my binary, either/or view of this treatment was kind of wrong. Well, actually, it was totally wrong. It seems that there are tons of possible outcomes, and while we did not get the best possible outcome, we probably didn't get the worst one either.

Kirsten still has palpable lumps in her breast. They are considerably smaller than they initially were, and the fact that they have shrunk so much seems to indicate that the high-dose chemo was, in fact, the way to go, since, as you may recall, the regular-dose chemo basically didn't do squat against this cancer.

The fact that they are still there does not indicate that we should stick a fork in her either. The hope at this point is that they will do a mastectomy, radiation, and that the PET scan will show that the stuff in her spine is gone. In any case they are starting her on some nonhormonal antiosteoporosis drug (did I mention that she came out of this treatment menopausal?) which also has been shown to retard cancer growth in bones.

Should her tumor markers begin to rise, they will start her on Herceptin, which may work as a kind of maintenance thing for years. It's only been around for four years so far, and some people in situations similar to Kirsten's have been on it for that long and are still kicking around.

We ask and ask about what if this and what if that, and finally Dr. J says she knows we want the certificate that says, "Certified, this Twenty-first day of February, 2001. Kirsten C. Shanks will live disease free for at least ten years!" but they don't give those out, even to the people who get complete remissions, and the bottom line is that we just don't know. What we do know is that she can take a breath for a while and relax and not worry about dying right now, and that's pretty much the best they can do.

It has to be enough, because it's all they have, and strangely enough, for both of us, it is. Like I said, I am sure I am not done with feeling depressed and angry about this, but I do feel in some important way that I have turned a corner. Maybe now I can get up more days than not and not worry about everybody dying. Maybe I can start keeping my own house clean. Maybe.

After she says that, she also clears Kirsten to do all the stuff she's been doing anyway, which is a relief.

We go out to lunch, and we stop by the thrift store run by the local AIDS charity, and they are selling vinyl records for a quarter. The fact that this is an AIDS charity—well, let's just say that there are a *lot* of Barbra Streisand albums (and what appears to be Dan Fogelberg's entire catalogue—who knew?), but I manage to pick up a stack of LPs from the 1980s that have one or two good songs on them, including Wham!'s *Make It Big,* which actually has several, but most notably "Freedom." Coincidences like this are almost enough to make me believe in an activist deity.

A week goes by, and I go back to work, and maintain my good mood and hopeful outlook despite having, on Wednesday, to literally spend two hours trying to untangle a three-way conflict that centered on whether someone did or did not say excuse me when they bumped into someone else. Mostly, though, I get psyched up for Kirsten's birthday party. A few weeks ago I thought it would be a good idea to have a party for Kirsten, since her birthday was going to coincide with the end of her treatment. We have been very low-key about our birthdays for several years, but this year I felt like we needed a celebration that Kirsten has come through her treatment, that she's still here, that I am happy she was born.

So I called all of our friends, and everybody said yes. Just about the only good side effect of her having cancer is that nobody could, in good conscience, turn down an invitation to this party.

I come home at the end of the day on Friday, which is Kirsten's actual birthday, and Kirsten's parents are here, and this proves fortunate, because some dumbasses have, for no apparent reason other than to be assholes, thrown a rock and broken a storm window on the first floor, and with Kirsten's dad here to help me, we are able to get the offending pane out and replaced without too much trouble. I think it says a lot about my new improved mental state that I just take care of this without lamenting my fate or getting so stressed out I feel like I need a nap. We all go out to our new favorite vegetarian Chinese restaurant, and I eat myself into a stupor. Appetizers, soup, entrées, what the hell, it's a party, right?

And I do feel like celebrating. Kirsten is really back. She has been taking Rowen to school this week, has been medically cleared to go where other humans are, has energy, and is feeling as close to normal as a bald woman can feel. We are still riding the wave of hope from last week's doctor's appointment, and it looks like we will be able to have periods of normalcy in our lives after all. I guess we have had to redefine what normal is, but that's okay.

Rowen has also been doing better. One of her teachers told us that she had said something about various things that would happen "when my mom comes alive again," and now, I guess, her mom has come alive again, and she is acting much more well behaved than she has in months. I didn't really notice at the time, but now that Rowen is feeling better, I look back at the time when Kirsten was in and out of the hospital and think that Rowen was unusually quick to tears, petulant, and cranky during the whole time. But then, so was I.

Saturday comes and Rowen says, "I want to help you get the cake! And we have to get balloons and decorations and hats!" I'm glad she said something, because I didn't even think of decorations, much less hats. As it turns out, we go to three stores and can't find party hats, but we do get streamers and balloons before picking up the cake, some seltzer, and some Rolling Rock (which I buy for the first time in ten years despite its vile flavor because it's Kirsten's thirty-third birthday and the bottles have the little inexplicable "33" on them), and we come home and start setting up the party.

Everybody shows up, and it starts out slowly in the living room but ends up taking over the living room and the kitchen, and this is pretty spectacular because a lot of weekends when we are going to bed at 9:00 on Saturday night, we feel like we don't have any friends, and it has been years since we had two rooms' worth of people in our house. I run around like crazy and eat way too much, and have two Rolling Rocks over the course of the afternoon and find that they are not as vile as I remembered, and I make sure to point out the little "33" to everybody, and nobody else seems to think it was especially clever of me to buy them. We tell people to come any time between 12:00 and 5:00, so most people come at 3:00 and stay till 7:00, and we have a great time.

At various points in the afternoon, people will sort of draw me aside and ask how Kirsten is and what we know about her prognosis, and I strangely do not find this annoying and don't mind telling them that we know the treatment worked, but we don't know exactly how well, that she is having a mastectomy in a couple of weeks, and that we hope that's it, but even if it's not, we are, as Dr. J told us, entering a new era of how we treat this disease, so there's a lot of hope and not much data, and that is just fine with both of us.

As Joe and Katy are leaving, Katy says, "You know a lot of really nice people," and I think it is true. This is not one of those parties where anybody leaves going, "Who was that dickhead who wouldn't shut up?" or something like that. (Unless they were talking about me, but I think I was running around too much to be really annoying.)

So now it is Sunday morning after the party, and, as I always do after I have eaten too much, I feel disgusting. I got lots of bread and appetizers from the local Indian restaurant and overindulged in those, and I also had three slabs of the cake, which turned out to be so dense that all matter and light were sucked into it. So I feel bloated, but most of all, I feel happy.

I am happy because Kirsten is thirty-three, we had a great party, I have friends I love, I can hear Rowen down the hall playing dress-up, and a light snow is falling. I am happy because I thought there was only one outcome to all this that was hopeful, when in fact there were many hopeful outcomes, and we seem to have one of those, and I think I'm not going to write about the PET scan or the mastectomy, because, well, everything that happens after this is basically postscript. Like I said, I know you want a definitive ending almost as much as I do, but it looks like medical science hasn't reached the point where we can get that. So here is the most important fact: Kirsten is alive today. So am I. So is Rowen. So, if you are reading this, are you. And I guess that has to be enough. Enjoy your day.

ABOUT THE AUTHOR

Brendan Halpin is an English teacher. He lives in Boston with his wife, Kirsten, and daughter, Rowen. *It Takes a Worried Man* is his first book.